THE ART OF TRUST

THE ART

OF

TRUST

Healing Your Heart
and Opening Your Mind

LEE JAMPOLSKY Ph.D.

Author of
HEALING THE ADDICTIVE MIND

Quoted material reprinted with permission from
A Course In Miracles, published by:
Foundation for Inner Peace, P.O. Box 1104,
Glen Ellen, CA 95442.

Cover & text designed by Ken Scott
Composition by STAR TYPE, Berkeley

Jampolsky, Lee L., 1957–
    The art of trust : healing your heart and opening your
mind / Lee Jampolsky.
        p.   cm.
    ISBN 0-89087-710-6 : $9.95
    1. Trust (Psychology) 2. Self-perception.
3. Peace of mind. 4. Interpersonal relations.
5. Jampolsky, Lee L., 1957–
I. Title
BF575.T7J36   1994
155.2'32—dc20   93-38547
                                                  CIP

First printing 1994

1 2 3 4 5 6 7 / 99 98 97 96 95 94

Manufactured in the USA

TABLE OF CONTENTS
PART I

PART II

ACKNOWLEDGMENTS

Trust has not come easy for me, and there have been many who have assisted me in my inner exploration to find it: first, my wife, Carny, whose patience has been endless and love unconditional. My daughters, Jalena and Lexi, who have shown me the natural state of joy and light that exists in us all. I am grateful, also, to my parents and to my brother, Greg, who have never stopped believing in me and who have been willing to assist me as an adult to heal childhood pain.

I am also grateful to Amanda Bostian and Callie Chappell Nicholas, who have both taught me that indeed the past can be healed. Endless gratitude to my agent, Joe Durepos. I also thank Sensei Julio Toribio, who has helped me to experience what was once stuck in my intellect. My deep appreciation to Dr. James Bugental for continuing to help me discover who I am.

Though at different times in my life I have immersed myself in the teachings of different world philosophers, in writing this book I found myself repeatedly returning to two for inspiration: Haridas Chauduri and J. Krishnamurti. Though few direct quotes from them appear in this book, in the writing of several sections of it, their works were consulted and contemplated.

I offer thanks to the many individuals who have chosen to share their lives with me during the process of intensive psychotherapy. The information in the vignettes of clients that I have included has been altered in order to ensure confidentiality. All names and identifying information have been changed. Many of the stories are composite sketches. Therefore, any resemblance that you may find between a vignette and the story of someone that you know is purely coincidental.

INTRODUCTION

There is purpose and meaning in everything that we do, in all situations that present themselves to us, and in all people who enter our lives. I truly believe that all of these aspects of life provide lessons for us to learn.

Still, learning these lessons is not always a straightforward task. When we continue to find ourselves unhappy in personal relationships, in work, and at home, we may begin to believe that positive change is impossible. This can be very self-defeating, draining our lives of necessary vitality.

In my personal journey and in my work as a psychologist, I have found that the issue of trust must be addressed before any deep and true change can occur in our lives. Trust is *the* core issue in the process of our personal growth.

Trusting ourselves implies knowing that we are fully capable and loving human beings. It means we acknowledge that fear is an illusion and love is real. Trust means that we do not impose limitations on ourselves or others, but rather that we always see growth and healing as available choices. It means that we stop blaming others and begin to embrace all of who we are. And trust requires that we recognize the interconnectedness of all life, and act accordingly. In short, when we are trusting, our inner guidance and outer actions are in accord: We live in harmony with ourselves, others, and our environment.

If an individual has difficulty trusting, this is more than likely because his or her view of the nature of trust is almost exclusively derived from painful past experiences. Unfortunately, many of us learned about the world from parents who were themselves untrusting. From an early age we hear many "don't trust" messages but very few "trust" messages. We hear, "Don't trust strangers," but rarely hear, "Trust yourself." We hear, "Lock your bike [house, door, car, or safe] so that you don't lose what you have," but rarely hear, "Unlock your heart so you will know more of who you are and what you have."

This book defines trust as the foundation to peace of mind; it defines fear as the state of *lacking* trust. Unfortunately, we have become more accustomed to being fearful than we have to trusting—a perilous habit, since trust and fear, like oil and water, never mix.

The purpose of this book is to offer you a means to know yourself better and to learn to trust what you know. It is not simply concerned with "achieving trust," but with the ongoing development of our ability to become loving, compassionate, and trusting human beings. With the ability to trust ourselves, others, and God, all else begins to fall into place in our lives.

Many of us share the common misconception that trust is something that we "get" only after we meet with the right person, or when life is going our way. This way of thinking goes, "If only I could find somebody to love me, then I could trust," or, "How can I possibly trust after all the terrible things that have happened to me?"

This book presents an alternative belief system. It states that we must first develop trust within ourselves before joy can consistently take root and blossom. It is the development of trust, and the traits that rest on trust, that this book addresses.

Failing to develop trust keeps our joy locked away. Fortunately, even when we do not consciously choose to develop trust, our mind still impels us to do so. Leading the development process in a conscious direction is a way of reclaiming our capacity for close relationships and a happy life.

In truth, our every thought and action either develops trust or inhibits it. If we want positive change in all aspects of our lives, we must:

- Explore the belief system which is the core of our distrust.
- Relinquish dysfunctional beliefs. Attempts at being trusting are destined for failure unless we are willing to look at who we are and what we believe.

Our capacity to love cannot be funneled into a romantic quest to find the right object to love or person to be loved by. Love begins within, and it is limitless. Our culture tends to teach the opposite: that trusting and loving are a result of finding the right person. The truth is that trust has more to do with *our own perception* than with another's behavior.

No greater art to be mastered rivals the ability to trust and to fully love. It is common to think that developing trust happens by chance—that there is nothing we can learn that will increase our success. This attitude needs to be changed if we are ever to realize our potential as human beings.

This book is presented in two sections. The first half focuses on the development of trust by identifying and discussing six steps one can undertake to become more trusting. The second half addresses the characteristics of love that can be developed, all of which rest upon trust.

Briefly, the six steps in developing trust are:

I: "THE PERIOD OF UNDOING"

Here, we develop the ability to examine how we think. We identify our basic beliefs and value system, and introduce some structural changes in our life.

II: "THE PERIOD OF SORTING OUT"

We begin to identify exactly which kinds of thoughts and behavior foster our peace of mind and which don't. We develop the ability to both make and trust our own decisions.

III: "THE PERIOD OF RELINQUISHMENT"

After the sorting out process, the next step is to get rid of the shame, guilt, and fear that bind us. Here the emphasis is upon letting go of these constructs.

IV: "THE PERIOD OF SETTLING DOWN"

The focus here is on consolidating our learning. Having begun to relinquish fear and shame, we can now begin to become more loving.

V: "THE PERIOD OF UNSETTLING"

This is a time where we learn to intently listen to our own inner wisdom and guidance.

VI: "THE PERIOD OF ACHIEVEMENT"

Generally, this is a time of more consistent peace of mind, and a time when trust, self-knowledge, and self-actualization often occur.

I was introduced to these steps and came to understand the kind of importance that trust occupies in our lives in reading and practicing *A Course in Miracles,* a three-volume self-taught course published by the Foundation for Inner Peace. Much of what I present in *The Art of Trust* is consistent with the thought system set forth in *A Course in Miracles.* Many of the lesson titles recall expressions from that set of volumes, printed here with permission of the holder of the copyright, its publisher. Where a term or phrase from *A Course in Miracles* is used, it will appear in quotation marks upon first appearance. Paraphrases are in single quotes. The location of the quoted material within *A Course in Miracles* is referenced in the Appendix.

The development of trust has been the doorway to change in my own life: Before learning to let go of my fear, happiness rested in a distant land and seemed unreachable. Absent of trust, my life was plagued by a void that I could never quite fill. I am still on the path of knowing myself; I still encounter fear. But each step becomes easier and more joyful as I release my fear and develop trust. It is with great respect for your own personal journey through life that I invite you to read and use this book.

PART

I

A
Different Perspective
on Trust

Psychoanalyst and teacher Erich Fromm said that the first step in positive change is the realization that love is an art. He wrote that if we want to learn to love, we should proceed in the same fashion that we would in learning any other art: by mastering the theory and practicing of it.

Mastering the art of loving is primarily the result of having learned the art of trust. Though the ability to more fully love may be seen as the larger goal of this book, our focus is clearly on the art of trusting.

Many of us see trust as the ability to be open and vulnerable with another person. Yet trust is much more than feeling safe from perceived judgment or abandonment by others. When thinking of trust, it's easy to mistakenly focus on the other person: Are they trustworthy? Have they hurt me before? Can they help me with my problems? Placing the emphasis outside of ourselves misses the true essence of what trust is: In developing trust we unlock the power and wisdom that is within us.

A-FRAME RELATIONSHIPS

Two people can become mutually dependent upon one another and mistakenly call the set-up a trusting relationship. I refer to this arrangement as an "A-frame relationship." If either side is moved, both sides fall, as in an A-frame structure. In my practice as a psychotherapist, I encounter this kind of relationship not infrequently. One such case involved a young couple who had come to sort out the kind of confusion and intense pressure this kind of arrangement can create.

When Bob and Mary came to see me they had been married for seven years. When asked why they were seeking help in their marriage, neither one could give a very clear answer. Mary, thirty-four, felt that she was leaving her youth with little sense of purpose in her life. Awkwardly smiling as she spoke in a calm voice, the space between Bob and her seemed to fill with tension.

Mary grew up in a wealthy area, but her family had been quite poor. She felt as though she never measured up to her peers. Mary's father left the family when she was four, leaving her mother to care for three daughters. Mary's mother worked as a waitress, and the family lived in a subsidized apartment. Her two sisters, who also felt they were not as important or valuable as their peers, became distant from their mother through rebellion. Meanwhile, Mary and her mother relied on each other for support and companionship. Mary began to believe that she and her mother had a "special bond," although neither had independence from the other.

During these years, Mary's mother was ill much of the time with vague physical complaints. Mary would listen to her for hours and felt special and needed because she did. Even in college, Mary relied solely on her relationship with her mother and never developed close friends. But around this time Mary began to realize that her mother was only interested in her own inner feelings, opinions, and thoughts. The unspoken agreement between them was that Mary would repress her own needs and emotions in exchange for feeling needed by her mother. Essentially, they were in an A-frame relationship; one in which each relied on the other but had little sense of identity or self-esteem of their own. One significant result of this arrangement was that

Mary came to believe that she needed someone else to focus on in order to feel whole.

Bob, now Mary's husband, came from a household with a different set of problems. Both of his parents were alcoholic, and his mother committed suicide when he was ten. His father raised Bob and a younger sister while working ten hours a day. Because Bob never had the opportunity to talk about his mother's death, he unconsciously looked for ways to ease that pain. He adopted the belief that being well-liked meant that everything was all right, and he became enormously popular in school.

As an adult Bob was very handsome and witty, yet had very little insight into himself. He remained emotionally distant from people even though he had many acquaintances. The two sides of the A-frame went up in record speed when he and Mary met. Bob saw that he could become "everything" to Mary. This allowed him to think to himself, "If I can make Mary unequivocally happy then I must be okay." Mary in turn believed, "With somebody as popular and confident as Bob, I won't need to relate with anybody else." It seemed to them that this was a match made in heaven.

But after seven years of marriage, though they couldn't describe it, they knew that something was wrong. In our work together their tasks were very similar. They each needed to reveal their pain of isolation and their fears of standing up on their own. In the process, they had to pull the two sides of the "A" apart and build a bridge between. Their task was to come to know and trust themselves, and to find genuine ways to share themselves with each other.

IDENTIFYING OBSTACLES TO TRUST

Bob and Mary's relationship provides just one example of how we must first develop trust within ourselves before we can discover peace of mind and have fulfilling relationships.

Though your life may seem quite different from Bob's and Mary's, ask yourself the following questions to unravel the similarities. Even though it may not seem readily apparent, trust issues are at the core of each of these questions.

1. Do you look to others for approval in order to feel good about yourself?
2. Do you have a difficult time knowing what you feel in certain situations?
3. Do you believe what others say, even when it results in your feeling shameful or guilty?
4. Do you believe that your happiness is dependent on having certain objects?
5. Do you have a difficult time making decisions and knowing what is right for you? Or, do you have a hard time being flexible once you have made a decision?
6. Do you look to relationships or work to make yourself feel whole?
7. Do you avoid relationships or certain situations because you fear rejection?
8. Once you decide something, do you constantly wonder if you made the wrong decision?
9. Do you feel that things "just happen" to you and that you have few choices in your life?
10. Do you feel uncomfortable in situations where you are not in control?

Yes answers are common, since most of us have some difficulties with trust. Sometimes we stop exploring trust at this point because the process all seems so overwhelming and confusing.

For years I myself danced around these questions. I avoided what was inhibiting trust in my life. Not unlike Bob, I was living a life that appeared full from the outside but lacked any experience of depth or fulfillment. I turned to money, drugs, and attractive women hoping that something would fill the void within me.

In the end, I felt as I might have if I had possessed a great-looking car that had no engine. I sat in my car smiling and waving to people, yet I wasn't going anywhere. Without trust my life had become frozen. Finally, I began to explore my inner life and to discover trust—the issue that would become central to my knowing myself and to having intimate relationships with others.

At different times I could have answered "yes" to all of the above questions. Currently one stands out for me. Question five asks two related questions, *"Do you have a difficult time making decisions and knowing what is right for you? Or, do you have a hard time being flexible once you have made a decision?"* Both questions are based upon a fundamental and underlying lack of trust.

At one time I had difficulty making decisions. Tired of my indecisiveness, I forced myself to make decisions, but I was inflexible in them. I thought that I solved the problem of being wishy-washy when I was able to make snap decisions and never waver. Both behaviors were opposite ends of a pole. They were fueled by the nagging voice in my head saying, "I cannot trust myself. I could be wrong, and if I am it would just prove how stupid I am." The following illustrates this process.

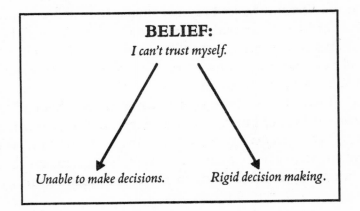

BELIEF:
I can't trust myself.

Unable to make decisions.   *Rigid decision making.*

In my early childhood my parents were very encouraging and supportive of my brother and me. As with most parents, mine were not perfect, but I have always known that they loved me. In supporting my growth, they communicated to me that I could do anything that I wanted to if I tried hard enough—a message that, surprising though it may seem, had both positive and negative implications.

When I started elementary school I had a speech impediment. Because of the teasing of the other kids, I soon became acutely self-conscious. When pronouncing any word containing the letter "s," I would make a "shh" sound. No matter how hard I tried to improve nothing seemed to work. I was soon in speech therapy and it was determined that the way my mouth had developed made it difficult for me to speak clearly.

In order to correct the problem I was fitted with a device that I was to wear in my mouth. This device was called a "prosthesis." Was this somebody's cruel idea of a joke? How could they give a child who can't say any "s" words a contraption called a prosthesis? Any attempt at pronouncing it meant sounding like I was trying to talk with a mouth full of grapes.

I have many memories of telling kids who were teasing me to shut up, only to have them reply, "*Shh*ut up yourself." Out of embarrassment, I wore the prosthesis only at night. As time went on I began to feel very angry.

I was at bat in a baseball game with a kid called Tiger on the mound. Teasingly, he began to make the "shh" sound over and over. In a rage I ran out to the mound and began to fight him. The parents in the bleachers were shocked. The coach and the other players had to pull us apart. As a result of my reaction, I ended up even more ashamed.

Slowly I was learning that what my parents had taught me, with the best of intentions, was not true. On the surface the message, "you can do anything if you try hard enough," appears positive. In actuality it has an element of "sweet poison" because it sets up an eventual failure. In my case it resulted in shame.

Until the physical structure of my mouth was changed, no matter how hard I tried I couldn't change my speech. I also began to get the message that my feelings were not acceptable and that my anger was inappropriate. I began to stop trusting myself, especially my thoughts and my feelings.

Eventually, the prosthesis combined with speech therapy worked. With some effort I was able to speak normally. What did not change was my feeling that I could not trust others or myself. At the time, I was never able to speak much about how I felt. I began to repress most of my uncomfortable feelings of discomfort.

As I grew older, I had difficulty making decisions because I had no clear sense of how I really felt, and because I wouldn't trust what I felt or thought, even if I did get a sense of it. This was not based solely on my speech problems as a child. It was not just that I felt I spoke differently from others. I felt that there was something fundamentally wrong with me. People who feel this way avoid making decisions, and that is exactly what I did.

I did poorly in high school and began to spend much of my time experimenting with drugs. Drugs seemed the perfect solution for avoiding making any decision or commitment. It is my belief that nobody recovers from any addiction without addressing the core issue of trust.

In my college years I believed that if I knew more I could make better decisions. Instead of addressing my trust issues I began to challenge other people. I thought that when I was a "good debater" that I would feel more powerful. I began to believe that if I could intellectually control and dominate people that I would feel secure.

I was wrong. I became opinionated and controlling. Feeling separate from others I began to isolate myself. As long as concepts like openness, trust, gentleness, and acceptance were ignored, decisions were easy to make. It wasn't until much later that I began to learn some simple truths:

1. Decisions based upon the need to control and dominate lead to feelings of isolation and separateness.
2. Decisions based upon trust lead to feelings of unity and compassion.
3. More information does not always lead to making positive life decisions.
4. Learning to quiet our minds and listen to our inner guidance ensures the ability to make decisions.

Much of my life I have been afraid. It was only when I had grown up and was attending graduate school that I began to find that there was another way of being in the world. Many of the courses I took were in Asian Studies. I began to be exposed to many Eastern and Western spiritual traditions. Simultaneously I was in a clinical psychology program studying many different personality theories and schools of psychotherapy.

In the course of these studies, I began to see that my life lacked an inner focus. I realized that it was difficult to trust a person I didn't know, and I didn't know myself. Compounding the problem, I was afraid of what I didn't know.

I began to study and practice various forms of meditation. I also entered psychotherapy. In retrospect, I believe that I was beginning to learn how to trust myself.

In order to develop trust I had to first become more conscious of my thoughts and my feelings. This was difficult because I had no awareness of my internal processes. I approached myself and the world with self-judgment and dogmatic criticism. Forgiveness must be seen as the highest of priorities if we are to love and trust. Knowing, loving, and trusting ourselves is the highest aspiration that we can realize.

Every step away from fear and darkness is a step towards love and acceptance. It is in this direction that we must choose to travel if we want self-knowledge. Peace of mind is awakened through developing a deep and complete sense of trust. The peace of mind that comes from trust is limitless in its depth. We always have the choice whether to listen to and trust the gentle voice of our inner guidance or the sharp voice of fear. Being able to choose between the two rests on the development of trust.

CHAPTER TWO

"The Period of Undoing"

The first stage in developing trust concerns the way in which we think. We begin this stage by examining the source or sources of our belief system. It is impossible to make lasting changes in our lives if we haven't adopted a willingness to explore our thinking and thought process. To do this we must be willing to look deeply at experiences in our lives that have contributed to our current value system.

The words "belief" and "value" are used extensively throughout this book, and the two are intimately connected. In the period of undoing, it is important to begin to understand the relationship between our beliefs, our values, and what we experience. All of the other periods of development address the interface of these three areas.

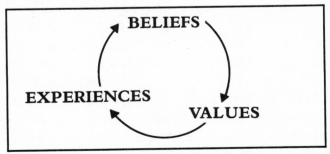

What we believe determines what we value, and our values influence what we experience. This process reinforces our original belief. This is a very important process to understand because our beliefs about who we are shape our experiences in life. The logical place to start with developing trust is to explore what we believe. The following parable helps to illustrate this process.

THE YOUNG MAN AND THE GARDENER

Imagine a young boy who has been told that if he plants some magic rocks in the earth, a tree will grow. He is told that this tree will bear fruit that will give him everything he needs. The boy *believes* that the rocks are his key to finding happiness, and he *values* them greatly. He ventures out and finds a small plot of soil that he feels will nurture his "seeds." He plants the rocks and waits for a sign of growth. He visits the plot day after day. He only finds that there is nothing but the dry dirt he left the day before.

As the boy grows older he begins to wonder why he is not growing the beautiful tree promised him. With each year he becomes more frustrated. Finally he ventures out to find a solution to his predicament.

The first person that he comes across is the gardener for the town park. He inquires about how to make plants grow. Being guarded about his magic seeds, he does not tell the man what he is trying to cultivate. The gardener tells him that for anything to grow well, it needs nurturing, plenty of water, and ample sun. "Well," the young man says to himself, "that is obviously the problem. The plot of land that I chose as a child was in the shade, and I had no idea that water was needed."

This new information depresses the young man because he has invested so much time in cultivating his tree. In the long run he is happy because he believes that it is simply the shady plot and lack of water that have caused his misfortune. He digs up his rocks and carefully replants them in a sunny spot, close to a stream where he can get plenty of water. Soon he begins to see some growth and is exhilarated. He continues to water the small green sprouts that he sees protruding from the soil. He knows that it will be only a matter of time before his tree is in full bloom.

One day the boy proudly takes the gardener out to show the man his sprouting tree. The gardener is a kind person who had always been delighted to help anybody who took an interest in the earth and plants. The young man beams with enthusiasm when the two arrive at the plot. The gardener does not know how to tell the young man that all this effort, water and sunlight has produced only weeds. There is no sprouting tree.

The weeds had reinforced the boy's belief that the rocks would grow his wonderful tree. The young man believes he is growing a magic tree, when the only thing emerging is weeds. Sadly, the boy has neglected all other areas of his life because he believes the rocks were of such great value.

Because the gardener is a man who believes in telling the truth, he tells the boy that his tree is still a long way from being realized. The gardener does not know that the seeds were actually rocks. He tells the boy that if he wants to have his tree grow, he will need to pull the weeds and clear the soil.

Initially, the boy finds this to be a painful task. He is being asked to pull up and throw away that which only a moment ago he had valued more than anything. The next day the gardener finds the boy pulling up the weeds and crying. The gardener is most impressed that the young man has had the courage to persevere throughout the many years. For this reason he decides to help the young man determine the problem.

The gardener asks the boy, "Where did you purchase your seeds, and what kind of tree are you trying to grow?" The young man guardedly replies that the seeds were rocks. "A man gave them to me when I was very small. He promised that the tree would give me everything I need in life."

The gardener has a dilemma. He can tell the boy that his seeds are merely everyday rocks, and that they will not grow anything. But he fears that this will surely break the boy's spirit. Conversely, if the gardener doesn't tell him, the boy will only go on valuing something that has no value. In the end, it seems to the gardener that the young man will be best served by knowing the truth, so that he may start over again and rebalance his life. After all, the boy has no friends; he has distanced himself from others. Because the child so believed that the tree would offer him everything, he nurtured no human friendships. He was certain that other people would want his tree for themselves.

With one hand, the gardener gathers up the rocks. The other, he rests on the young man's shoulder. He gently tells the young man the truth. How painful it is for the young man to hear that the tree he believes caused him to endlessly search for an answer would never grow. He has put all of his energy into something valueless and he becomes angry about all the time that he has wasted. More than anything, the young man is hurt that he has been deceived.

For a moment he wonders if the gardener is telling him the truth. He conjectures that perhaps the gardener wants the seeds for himself. Still, these thoughts pass, and the young man realizes that his belief has caused him to feel isolated and alone. If we were to chart it, the process would look like this:

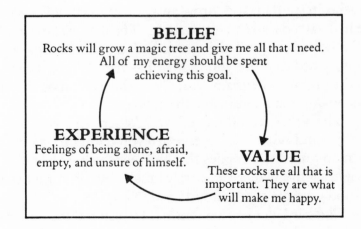

BELIEF
Rocks will grow a magic tree and give me all that I need.
All of my energy should be spent
achieving this goal.

EXPERIENCE
Feelings of being alone, afraid,
empty, and unsure of himself.

VALUE
These rocks are all that is
important. They are what
will make me happy.

The boy sees that as long as he continues to believe that the rocks are magic seeds, his sad life will never be any other way.

He must also come to grips with the fact that there will be no tree that will provide him all that he needs in life.

The gardener, being a wise and learned soul, begins to take long walks with the young man. He helps the boy see that he must nurture and care for himself if he is to find peace of mind.

The boy slowly enters a period of undoing his old way of thinking, which requires him to examine his beliefs. It is not a painless process, but for the first time the boy is stepping out of the dim atmosphere of false beliefs and into a new world of light and hope.

This parable illustrates many factors that are key to the period of undoing, some of which deserve more elaboration.

THE PAIN OF UNDOING BELIEF SYSTEMS

When the drug is taken away from the addict, that person experiences some pain and discomfort. This is not because the removed substance is "good" for them. Rather, the addict has become so used to the drug that the body and mind *believe* that it is needed.

We become addicted to our beliefs in the same way. Even if we identify beliefs that continually lead us into conflict and inner turmoil, we can experience deep loss and pain when we try to give them up. Our minds become "addicted" to thinking in certain ways. When we try to change we often are faced with great resistance. For this reason the period of undoing can be very difficult. Often, individuals give up before they get started.

Harry was forty-two years old when he came to see me. He was experiencing problems in his second marriage and was dissatisfied with his job. Though he was a bright man, Harry had never had a job that was anything more than menial. He and his wife seldom communicated any feelings to one another. Most of their time was spent in front of the television. Harry felt that his life was void of any meaning. He said that he never seriously thought of suicide before, but sometimes he wondered if there was really any way that his life could ever be satisfying to him. It soon became clear that Harry had adopted many beliefs about himself that limited his ability to feel joy in his life. Below I outline three core beliefs that Harry adopted. In italics, I briefly state the origins of the belief.

1. I am never going to amount to anything. I should know by now that I screw up everything that I try to do. *Harry's father was always critical of him. No matter how well Harry did as a child, his father would tell how Harry could do it better.*

2. Communication should be kept to a minimum. I should always question what I feel. *Harry's parents "co-existed" but never expressed any verbal or physical warmth. Most emotion was expressed as anger. If Harry expressed a feeling or an opinion that was unpopular, he was met with condemnation.*

3. I don't have any control or choices in my life. *Harry saw all members of his family as unhappy, resentful, rageful, and fearful. He concluded that this was a result of external circumstances beyond their control. He saw their reactions as "normal."*

These beliefs led Harry to a life devoid of aliveness, which he described. If he were to uproot these beliefs by exploring his inner world he would undoubtedly live a fuller life. However, the period of undoing is not always so simple, because we create obstacles and fears that thwart our inner exploration. In fact, the origin of the belief is not as important as confronting and working through these obstacles. Simple insight into the beginning of a belief does not necessarily lead to deep change.

Below, I identify the "healthy alternative" to each of Harry's core beliefs. In italics I describe the resistance that Harry encountered in letting go of the old belief. The necessary approach to deep change is one that gives value to the new belief and encourages working through old fears:

> **New Belief:** I am a capable human being.
> Should I make a mistake, it is simply an
> opportunity to learn.
> **Obstacle:** *If I see myself as capable, that will
> mean that I will have to begin to take some risks.
> Other people will see my mistakes as failures.*

> **New Belief:** Letting others know who I
> am will allow me to know myself. I trust my
> feelings and my intuition.
> **Obstacle:** *If I let others know me I will be
> abandoned.*

> **New Belief:** I can always choose how I feel,
> what I believe, and what I value. The situation
> is not the determinant of my experience.
> **Obstacle:** *Taking responsibility for my thoughts
> and actions means I can no longer blame others or
> be a victim.*

All of the above obstacles can be seen as *resistances.* They illustrate the "fear factor" within our thinking. In his particular case, Harry's original thinking is causing him pain, yet he continues to think in the same dysfunctional ways. This is because his ego tells him that change is dangerous. As a result, change is perceived as being frightening.

Our resistances scream, "Help me to change, but please don't make me give up anything." In the period of undoing we may feel that we are being asked to give up something useful. At this stage of developing trust, we don't yet understand that we are not giving up anything useful to our growth. On the contrary, in order to continue, one must fan the spark of faith that a better life is possible.

CORE BELIEF EXERCISE

On a sheet of paper list all of the aspects of your life that you feel are not as you would like them to be. Be specific. Don't just write, "My relationship with my partner is bad," but rather, list very detailed ways that illustrate your feelings.

Begin to think about what the core beliefs are behind the experience, as I did with Harry. For example, if you stated, "I don't get enough recognition for my work," ask yourself, "Do I believe that I am worthwhile? Do I believe that it is unattractive to be assertive?" Even in areas of your life where you feel comfortable, list the aspects that are less than desirable. Do not rush through this. Spend some time each day for about a week.

Some suggested areas to focus on are: work, relationship with partner (or lack of a relationship), relationship with parents, social life, sexuality, spirituality, intellectual life, feeling life, body image. When you are all done make a title page for your work. The title page should say:

> **The Following Are the Effects of My Present Way of Thinking. If I Want To Change These Aspects of My Life, I Will Need To Undo My Present Belief System And Be Willing to Work Through My Fear.**

THE GENUINE DESIRE TO CHANGE VS. THE MAINTAINING OF SURFACE GOALS

Before we can change we must first have a sincere desire to change. This may seem obvious, yet most of the people who fall short of their goals do so for straightforward reasons. Most of these have to do with what I call "surface goals."

To show clients how to distinguish a surface goal from a desire for deep change, I sometimes use the metaphor of remodeling a home. A few years back I decided to do some remodeling on our house. The original structure itself was quite old and was never really intended for year-round use. For this reason, the foundation was essentially nonexistent, and the quality of the original lumber was poor. My goal was to upgrade the house.

Like most home owners, I didn't want to spend much money. The contractor told me if I added on without addressing the core problems, I would most likely have larger problems in a few years. He suggested that I redo the whole structure. Naturally this was met with resistance on my part. I had a "surface goal" of just fixing the place up so it looked better from the outside. Eventually, because of the contractor's patience and persistence, I conceded and we now are much happier because of it. Knowing that our house doesn't just look good, but is also structurally sound gives me great peace of mind.

Surface goals usually have to do with external appearances. They lead to surface change that is rarely lasting in any enduring way. In order to make any deep change, we must first truly commit to developing ourselves into more trusting human beings.

To acquire this depth of motivation and commitment, we must recognize the lack of value in our present belief system. This process is an essential aspect of developing trust. It is also often met with tremendous resistance. None of us wants to discover that the way we think is dysfunctional. Most all of us are very attached to the way that we think and our value system. When it is threatened in any way we become very defensive. In fact, virtually all conflict (on both the personal and societal levels) is born out of this very phenomenon.

Sometimes it is easier to see resistance to positive change in the international sphere than it is to see it within our own lives. We can all remember the 1989 uprising begun by students in Tiananmen Square in China. A struggle for freedom from oppression can surely be seen as a move toward positive change. The Chinese government, however, responded to that move with great violence. This resistance to positive change stemmed from a fear of a new and different way of thinking.

In Beijing that fall, despite the difficulty, some young

men and women persevered in their quest for freedom: In one of the photographs, a single student stands in front of a tank, stopping it in its tracks. It is an image that will stay with me for years to come.

For me, that scene has served as a metaphor. It reminds me of how I have struggled internally, and how often I have given in to the oppressive ego in my mind. I know that I have sometimes run when my ego threatened me with the darkest of possibilities should I change my beliefs.

I have come to realize that we need to be as fearless and determined as that single student. We need to stand in front of all of our fear, saying, "Stop, there is a better way."

If we are not experiencing trust, love, and compassion in a consistent way in our lives, it can only be for one reason. Our belief system is such that we continually invest our time and energy in areas that repeatedly lead to conflict, separation, and fear.

BRINGING NEWNESS TO RELATIONSHIPS

Open-mindedness comes from committing yourself to seeing things differently. When we choose to see any one thing differently, all of our thinking is affected. It does us no good to have "limited open-mindedness." When we place limits on our vision, it is because we have fear and a lack of trust in our hearts. If we feel compelled to stand firm on "knowing all and being right," it is because we are really afraid of something.

My wife, Carny, and I have a relationship in which we are both committed to learning and growing—both as individuals and as a couple. This does not mean that we are conflict free. There are occasions when I react to her and it may appear that I don't practice what I preach. But Carny and I see each other as human beings, and we humans are vulnerable to mistakes. She and I try to see mistakes as an opportunity to learn.

One of my most common mistakes is reacting to Carny as if I know what she is thinking, and believing that her thoughts are a judgment or criticism towards me. Then I respond defensively, thinking that I will become "safer" if I put up a wall.

Sometimes I even go so far as to tell her what she is thinking and that I am upset about it. I might say something like: "You're not telling me that you're angry about this. I know that you are because you are not saying anything to me." I am under the impression that her silence is hiding a negative feeling towards me. The truth is that she may simply need some quiet time. Instead, I find myself telling her about herself instead of *asking* her to tell me.

In truth, I am mistaken when I believe that love means that I know Carny in all aspects. The following elaborates.

> *Loving someone is recognizing that you can always deepen your understanding of who that person is.*
>
> *Loving someone is about sharing who you are and listening to who that person is with the ear of the heart rather than the ear of judgment. Love means that we are always willing to let go of the past.*
>
> *Loving someone is allowing the present moment to bring new and unlimited awareness of who you are, who that person is, and who you are together.*
>
> *Whenever you are thinking judgmentally about someone, remind yourself:*
>
> *Hidden beneath all of my ideas and preconceived thoughts is something of beauty; clean, and of infinite value.*

We are beginning to discuss how we may change our perception of a situation or person in order to experience compassion and love. Following are the tasks that assist us in changing perception.

TASK 1: RECOGNIZING VALUE
AND LACK OF VALUE

The essential phase of the period of undoing has to do with recognizing beliefs that lead to our valuing that which lacks value. In the parable of the young man and the gardener, deep change was impossible for the young man until he recognized the inherent problems in his belief system. He could follow endless surface goals, such as finding a perfect growing site, but until the core of his faulty belief system was recognized, he would only find failure.

Each of us, right now, has a specific view of the world and ourself. These ways of seeing are like various lenses we see through. We will call these ways of seeing "schemas." Some schemas lead to a sense of inner calm, self-esteem, and peace of mind. Other schemas lead to tension, low self-worth, constant fear, and lack of trust.

After achieving the desire to change, the next step is to begin to acquire the skills to determine which schemas are "valuable" (positive) and which are "valueless" (negative). What has true value leads to peace of mind. Conversely, what is valueless leads us to conflict.

One negative schema that I have fallen prey to in the past is what I call my "Not Enough Thinking" schema. When I am entrenched in this schema I feel that no matter what I do, I'll never be sufficient. At the same time, I assume that I am being totally rational and logical. It always starts when I dig into my past or I project into the future. The past is over and does not now exist. The future is not yet here, and does not exist in this moment either. Thus, with the Not Enough Thinking schema, I am basing an entire thought system on things that do not exist. This is hardly rational.

In our culture, the Not Enough Thinking schema is most commonly manifested in one of two ways: *love*—feelings of not having enough love are prevalent throughout society today;

and *money*—a great percentage of us state that we don't really have enough money and that more would make us happier.

When I went to college at age eighteen, I had a very difficult time adjusting; in fact, I had never felt quite so alone. Looking back, I see that it was the point at which I began to experience the aloneness that I had always repressed.

My way of dealing with this overwhelming aloneness was to become compulsive in my studies. I did very little else. When I did do something socially, I felt out of place and extremely awkward. Other people seemed to have an ease about them that I didn't have. Fear began to be my constant companion. I became convinced that I was different than others and that I would never be able to have "normal" relationships. I longed for acceptance and love, yet felt that I was unlovable.

As the years went on, burying myself in books did not seem to be easing the pain. I felt that love had somehow passed me by. I began to loathe the way I was, yet saw no other way of seeing myself or the world. My only reprieve was in the use of drugs.

The drugs gave me a feeling of psuedo-warmth, an imitation version of the warmth that was missing in my life. Narcotics became my substitute for love. My trust of others all but vanished. The only thing that I trusted was the belief that I was never going to have intimate and close relationships. I projected this belief into the future so well that I, for a time, became completely isolated.

One day a glimmer of hope arrived. I started to believe that my life could be another way. This thought did not come without pain, however. In fact, I had no idea what it was that I could do to change my circumstances. After a few days, it became clear that if I wanted change in my life, I was going to have to trust another person; my only other option was to die. Despairingly, I took the first step and told my brother, Greg, part of the story of my hidden pain and drug use. At the time, I didn't open up completely, but it was the beginning of change.

I firmly believe that to reverse a Not Enough Thinking perspective, we only need to begin to entertain the idea that the world is a safe place. This leads to seeing that we are actually full of love and can simply allow it to be itself. Even the dimmest light in a dark room transforms the darkness. Telling my brother part of my secret pain was a small spark of light. It began to reverse the process:

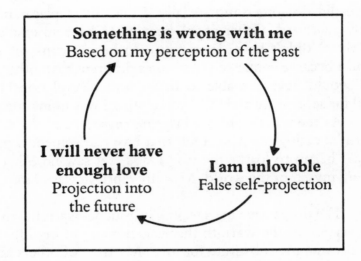

It is impossible to trust as long as we create a false and negative self-perception and project it into the future. Not Enough Thinking is only one example of a negative schema that leads us into pain. Although the list of possible negative schemas is endless, the following are five of the most common I have come across. (In italics is the experience that results from giving value to these false thoughts. Remember, negative schemas lead us into "valuing the valueless," which leads us into negative experiences.)

NEGATIVE SCHEMAS AND
THE EXPERIENCES THEY PRODUCE

People are out to get me. It's a dog-eat-dog world. If I don't look out for myself, nobody else will.

I am always suspicious and rarely trusting. I can't trust love. I don't allow anybody to become close to me. I feel alone most all of the time, but I would never admit it.

My self-esteem is based upon looking good in the world. It is more important to keep up a good front than to let anybody know how I feel.

I am preoccupied with my body image. I tend to be a workaholic, and I'm possibly prone to chemical dependency. My relationships are primarily superficial. When somebody does begin to get close I usually feel inadequate and do something to sabotage the closeness.

I follow the adage, "The one who dies with the most toys wins." Material possessions will make me happy. The more I have, the better I will feel.

I never feel fully adequate because there is always something else to be acquired. I have only momentary happiness when something is new, and then there is something else to get. I compare myself with others all of the time.

My achievements are who I am. The more I achieve, the better I am.

I am constantly chasing some sort of goal. When I achieve it, I have only momentary satisfaction, if that. If I am not getting external validation, I don't feel worthwhile. My relationships are usually based on my being dominant and controlling. If I am not in control I don't feel very safe.

I am a victim of the world. Bad things always happen to me. People always try to take advantage of me.

I always feel as though the world is against me. Because I believe that I am a victim, I feel like one. I tend to be a chronic blamer. I feel that things just "happen" to me. I have no control over my life. I take no responsibility for my life.

TASK 2: ADOPTING AN OPEN ATTITUDE— CHANGING PERCEPTION

If we want to learn to recognize what is valuable and what is not, we must begin to learn how we use negative schemas. At this time, it is not important to identify and analyze all of your schemas. It is more important that you begin to recognize the following whenever you are in pain:

"There is another way of looking at the world."

To the closed, conflicted, and arrogant mind this statement means nothing. The closed and untrusting mind says:

There is only one way to see things,
and my way is right.

Our thinking determines the degree to which we are able to trust. If we want to trust, we must be willing to become more flexible in our thinking. In the past, when I viewed the world in a black-and-white way, I believed that my negative self-image was accurate. I failed to see that my perception was based upon a distorted memory of my past experiences. As a result, I carried around the weight of shame.

In order to heal this shame, I have had to be willing to bring up these past situations to conscious awareness, change my perception of them, and then release them through forgiveness. The following account illustrates this point.

Our experiences when we are growing up shape our perception of ourselves. Often we carry feelings for years that are a result of what others have told us about ourselves.

When I was a sophomore in high school, I chose to go to a private school. My parents agreed. My freshman year in a public school had been difficult for me socially and academically, and I looked forward to being in a different environment.

About half way through my sophomore year, my parents decided to get divorced. I began to repress a lot of the feelings I had about this. In retrospect, I think I probably tried to keep my parents together by having the focus of attention on me. I faked accidents and illness in a desperate attempt to "do something" to keep them together, although none of this behavior was entirely conscious at the time.

The school I was attending emphasized extracurricular activities. There were also high expectations of student academic performance. I, however, was so preoccupied with my parents that I rarely did any of my schoolwork. As a result I dreaded going to my classes: I knew that I would feel dumb and ashamed.

My involvement with the after-school activities was minimal. The inner pain that I was experiencing remained locked inside and only seemed to get worse as the year progressed. The curious thing was that school was also more comfortable than home that year. School became a place where I felt that I could trust others. I never really talked to any of the teachers, but I did feel that there were some that understood my hidden pain.

At the end of the school year I was called into the headmaster's office. I was told that I was being expelled. I was shocked. I was told that I was not welcome back because I "was not the caliber of student that they wanted." They further stated that they attributed my behavior and lack of abilities to my dealing drugs on campus. I had never done this and the suggestion of such only added to my feeling misunderstood and alone. At the time I had a terrible temper from all of the repressed feelings. My response was yelling, slamming the door, and screeching off in my car.

For many years this experience deeply affected me. We tend to act according to what we believe. I believed the headmaster's assessment of me and really thought that I was not very intelligent or worthwhile. I never did very well the rest of high school. I did become involved with drugs and increasingly unaware of who I was. My potential as a human being remained hidden.

In my senior year (back at public school), I became involved with some other students in personal awareness activities led by a man named Paul Erlich, who later became a friend. These activities introduced me to awareness, growth, and communication and—for the first time—I began to see that there was some hope for me. Maybe, just maybe, I was a worthwhile human being.

Whenever we believe we are anything other than lovable, worthwhile, and complete, it is an indication that we are believing in a false perception of ourselves. As an adult I have chosen to change my past-based perception of who I thought I was. In the school example, this process of change looked like:

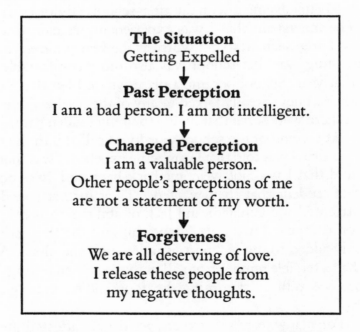

The Situation
Getting Expelled
↓
Past Perception
I am a bad person. I am not intelligent.
↓
Changed Perception
I am a valuable person.
Other people's perceptions of me
are not a statement of my worth.
↓
Forgiveness
We are all deserving of love.
I release these people from
my negative thoughts.

Changing our perception is not only applicable to past experiences, it is also very useful in helping us to live life from day to day. When any situation arises in which you are tempted to become angry, guilty, shameful, or upset, state clearly to yourself:

I can choose to change my perception of this.

TWO ASPECTS OF THE MIND

When we say, "There is another way of seeing this situation," we are beginning to indirectly ask a part of our mind to be exercised that has long been dormant. There are two aspects of our mind that we always choose between. One is the "Ego Mind." The other is the "Whole Mind."

The Ego Mind, or ego, is based on fear. It constantly searches for past experiences to reinforce its beliefs that we are something other than whole. Simply put, the ten commandants of the Ego Mind are:

1. Fear is real.
2. Guilt is good.
3. The past is the basis of reality.
4. The future should be controlled.
5. I am fundamentally alone.
6. Defense and attack create safety.
7. Judgment leads to change.
8. Comparison is helpful.
9. Being right is important.
10. Blame makes me feel better.

The Whole Mind, or our "inner guidance," is based on love. The Whole Mind recognizes the interconnectedness of life. It is the source of compassion. The ten commandments of the Whole Mind are:

1. Love is the core of who we are.
2. "Forgiveness is the key to happiness."
3. The present moment is the genuine basis of reality.
4. Choice is always with us.
5. We are a part of all life.
6. Extending compassion always results in something positive.

7. Acceptance leads to change.
8. Seeing commonalities creates closeness with others.
9. Being happy is important.
10. We are responsible for how we feel.

No matter how much we believe it to be true, it is never external circumstances that determine what our inner experience is. When you come home and say to your spouse, "Boy, did I ever have a bad day," the automatic response is usually "What happened?" Though this may be helpful, because listening is always useful, it is asking the wrong question. In asking "What happened?", we are reinforcing the belief that circumstances are responsible for how we feel. The more appropriate response—even though it sounds awkward—would be, "What were you believing today?"

No matter what the circumstances, we are still responsible for our peace of mind. We are responsible for each and every thought that we have. We are not robotic computers that have no choice but to react as programmed. Our reactions and what we experience are dependent upon which aspect of the mind we are utilizing.

When we say, "There is another way of looking at the world," we are talking about shifting from the Ego Mind to the Whole Mind. The voice of the ego does not give up without a fight, however. When we begin to quiet our thoughts, the Whole Mind begins to guide us in our affairs. It is often difficult after years of trusting the loud voice of the ego to begin to trust the gentle voice of our inner guidance. Making this shift can truly be seen as the process of learning to trust ourselves.

More precisely, "trusting ourselves" means learning to distinguish between the Ego Mind and the Whole Mind. We are always either trusting the ego or the Whole Mind—for the two cannot co-exist.

Carla was a young woman who I had the opportunity to work with in psychotherapy for some time. From an external perspective, her life was "in order" when she first came in to see me. She had a good job in the business world; she did not live beyond her means; she had a boyfriend of four years and seemed to have many friends. Despite all of this, it appeared that Carla had been unhappy and confused most of her life.

Carla had little parental support while she was growing up. It wasn't that her parents were absent or fighting all the time. It was simply that Carla was the youngest of five children, and she became the "invisible" child. She was the one who didn't need a lot of input. She was never particularly bad or particularly talented at anything. She was always average, never standing out in any way.

As she explored her inner world she found that a deep feeling of aloneness had been with her as long as she could remember. Even when she was with her friends, there was still a part of her that felt alone. As time went on, she found that she never really thought that her parents wanted her. She felt that she wanted to apologize for her existence. In all of her relationships with people, she felt that she was never really fully accepted. She believed that she was better off by keeping people at a certain distance.

By developing her trust in the Whole Mind, Carla was able to see herself as a person who had a lot to offer the world. She began to see that she was a valuable person.

TASK 3: RECOGNIZING THAT THE EGO'S WAY HASN'T WORKED

Recognizing that the ego's way hasn't worked is often one of the most difficult steps in changing our perception and adopting a trusting and loving thought system. It is difficult because it is essentially saying that the way of the ego has not served us. The ego is like a rebellious child who begins to kick and scream when attention is not paid to it.

The ego's means of undermining trust is to constantly evaluate, compare, judge, criticize, project, condemn, manipulate, shame, and instill guilt. Before we can find peace of mind, we must fully come to recognize that these means never get us what we want. When the ego sees that it is losing ground, it will sometimes try to convince us that aspects of its ways should be retained. The ego claims: "In this situation, you better rely on the past; remember, you were hurt before." Or, "I shouldn't trust that I like those people, I have heard bad things about them."

So this third task on the way to changing our perception requires us to *fully* understand and see clearly that the means of the ego *never* result in peace of mind.

You cannot be successful when you have split goals. Wanting all that trust offers while still placing value in the ego will constantly result in shooting yourself in the foot.

This step is best reinforced when we take some time to examine all the occasions that we have turned to the ego for guidance. By so doing, we can begin to see that there is no value in what the ego offers.

I invite you to do the following exercise. It is important that you spend adequate time doing this task. As long as you place value in the ego's thought system, it will be difficult for you to see the use of the rest of this book.

On separate sheets of paper address the following. (For clarification I have included, in italics, one example from my own life for each task.)

1. List at least ten times in your life that you have judged others for what they have done. Include any and all grudges that you currently hold.
   (Example: Last month when my wife didn't make a particular phone call, I judged her as being irresponsible. I still hold a grudge, even though up to now I have not talked about it with her.)
2. List at least ten occurrences in which you have judged yourself as being inferior, dumb, unlovable, and so on.

*(Example: During my divorce, I thought that
I was a bad person and was unworthy and incapable of having a lasting, loving relationship.)*

3. List at least five ways that you are afraid of
   the future because of something that
   occurred in the past.
   *(Example: I have been afraid that I wouldn't
   have enough money because of the years that
   I saw others being fearful about money.)*

4. List at least five times that you became
   defensive with someone close to you.
   *(Example: Last week I became snappy with my
   wife when I jumped to conclusions and thought
   she was saying that I was not doing a good job
   with the baby.)*

5. List at least five occasions that you have
   used guilt, shame, or intimidation, to try
   and get what it is you wanted.
   *(Example: A few years ago in disciplining an
   employee, I wanted them to feel guilty for what
   I thought they had done so that they would
   perform better.)*

6. List not less than five occasions that you
   have held on to shame.
   *(Example: I believed that there was something
   wrong with me when I was kicked out of high
   school.)*

Now go over all of your work. Ask yourself the simple
question: Have any of these ways of thinking or actions ever
resulted in peace of mind? I am quite sure that your answer will
be "no."

After doing this exercise spend a few days frequently
reminding yourself:

*The way of the ego does not work. I am ready
to change.*

INTERNAL VS.
EXTERNAL CHANGES

Once we have recognized that the ego has not brought us anything other than pain, we can then see the value of the thought system that stems from the Whole Mind. Here we begin to make changes in our lives that reflect our inner calling to listen to the Whole Mind. Ultimately, we must make some fundamental shifts in our beliefs and values, which will lead to an inner shift of our perception. Interestingly, I have found that sometimes external shifts in the structure of what we do can indeed help us move toward this inner shift: Creating external changes can be likened to "setting the stage" for deeper internal change. We must remember, however, that external changes alone are insufficient.

Several years ago I was working as a hospital administrator. I had some clinical contact, but I had become more of a supervisor and paper-pusher. Though many people enjoy this type of work, I felt my desire to do psychotherapy was being traded in for a job working with paper. It seemed that I did my tasks because I was "supposed" to do them, rather than feeling that I was making any real difference in people's lives.

Although I wasn't enjoying the work, I was making more money than I had ever made before. For the first time in my life, I felt that I was not constantly worried about finances. My alternative was to go into private practice and to write. I wanted the change, but deep down I believed I couldn't really succeed. Staying in the position that I had was clearly allowing me to avoid the following fears:

The Fear of Failure
I feared that I would not find financial success, and I believed that this would prove my secret fear true: that I was not a good psychologist.

The Fear of What Others Think
I believed I was lucky to have landed the job that I did, and I was sure people would think I was

crazy to leave such a secure position. People would think I was grandiose and naive if they knew I left a well-paying job to try to write a book.

The Fear of My Dysfunctional Self Being Revealed
I had been hiding behind the prestige of my position, and feared having to be just "plain ol' Lee." I still didn't feel confident about myself, and so having something that made me look good was a "secure" feeling. (This type of "security" generates underlying insecurities. We feel that if we are "found out," our true dysfunctional self will be revealed.)

The Fear of the "Facts"
I looked around and saw other psychologists struggling in their practices. I feared that I would be like them. (I didn't spend much time looking at all of the financially successful psychologists who were not struggling. The Ego Mind always looks for what will reinforce fear, not dispel it.)

The Fear That All Mistakes are Permanent
I projected my fear so far into the future that I thought: "After I fail at this, then I will never be able to get another job, not even the same one I have and don't like now."

In this case, making an external change in my work situation (leaving the hospital) set the stage for me to move through some old fears. If we see fear as real and allow it to rule our lives, trust becomes impossible.

On the other side of fear, trust awaits us.

I did leave my job and I did struggle through my fears. What I found was, as my belief system changed, I had all of the work that I needed. The more I trust in myself and my inner process, the more I see that my work follows my needs. When I am feeling tired or stressed, my practice slows down a little. When I feel I would like to be working a lot, work somehow appears. This has happened so many times through the years, I can no longer write it off as coincidence. If I am attuned to what my needs are and what I am feeling—and if I believe I can truly live a life of balance—then this is exactly what I create for myself.

If you find yourself fearful of making some external change, work through the fear. You don't even have to make the change. It is overcoming the fear that is important. Fear is like a cement wall with barbed wire atop, keeping trust from us. As you begin to move through and beyond your fear, trust increases in our lives.

THE POWER OF THOUGHT

The power of thought is the most powerful tool that we have. It is also one we quickly discount. In one way, this book is really about the power of thought. The power of thought is central to the preceding story about my job change. It was the power of my negative thoughts that kept me bound in fear and in a job I didn't like. It is the power of my positive thoughts that creates freedom in my life.

Pete was a patient I saw for some time. He originally came to see me after completing an alcohol treatment program; he wanted to stay clean and sober. During the time that I saw Pete, he made some very profound changes: he became more fully able to trust himself, and to give and receive love. The work that he did in therapy was far beyond what he had imagined, for when he started out, he believed all he needed to do to make his life a happy one was not drink anymore.

At fifty-three, Pete had proven himself extremely successful in his career as a research chemist with his own pharmaceutical company. Yet being trained as a scientist limited Pete in some important ways; subjective experience, for example, made very little sense to him. If something could not be objectively quantified, he was not much interested in it, and had a difficult time believing it existed. And when it came to realizing the power of his own thinking, we might as well have been talking about invisible fairy godmothers. As I've said, Pete was much more interested in "tangible things"—since his thoughts could not be directly measured, he did not see how changing his thinking could make a difference in his life.

When he first came to see me, his identity was tied to his company's success, his money, and the long list of awards and publications. His thoughts seemed of little importance to him.

One day, after many sessions, Pete took an unexpected turn. Following weeks of visible progress, he seemed to be methodically reverting to his old patterns. Though he did not return to drinking, he began to see his life goal as one of achieving more accomplishments. He gave up his goal of choosing peace of mind. He was back into his objective and scientific mind. Rather than fight it, I began to enter into his objectified world to see if change could occur at that level.

Pete was obviously under great stress because of the return to his old ways of thinking. I asked him if he would be interested in being hooked up to biofeedback machines—devices that feed back our less conscious physiological responses, such as skin temperature and brainwave activity. I explained that they would graphically demonstrate his heart-rate, blood-pressure, galvanic skin response, skin temperature, and brainwave pattern. I wanted to help Pete see, in objective terms that appealed to his scientific mind, that his thoughts did have a direct effect on his ability to relax and be happy.

Being a scientist, this fascinated him. Once connected to the machines, he saw that his thoughts and way of thinking were in fact causing objective physiological responses. The data painted a picture of an individual under enormous pressure. He began to see that all the biofeedback instruments were doing was objectifying the results of his thinking. It was clear that they were revealing his obsessive "workaholic" way of thought.

Though I seldom work in such a strict cognitive fashion, I began to ask him questions about the general condition of our world. I asked him why he thought there were wars. We discussed family discord in general, as well as the building of nuclear weapons. We talked about the current ecological problems and their possible solutions. And finally we spoke of his life. Slowly, over a few months, he was able to discover that all of these things have one thing in common. They result from a certain and specific way of thinking. At last Pete began to see how every thought he has holds the power to create.

If we want to change our lives, we must recognize that it is with our thoughts that we must work. The simple statement, *our thoughts create,* must be fully accepted and embraced. Only then are we able to understand how our lives work and take responsibility for ourselves. Only then are we empowered.

CHAPTER THREE

"The Period of Sorting Out"

In the period of undoing, we learned that examining our beliefs and making changes in our external and internal lives can lead to increased trust. Having learned this, we must now begin to make decisions about what is or isn't helpful in this pursuit. Indeed, determining what is helpful to our peace of mind can be seen as the primary goal of the period of sorting out. During this period, decision making is one of the primary tasks.

THE EGO MIND'S WAY OF MAKING DECISIONS

When we ask the question, "Was 'x' a good decision?" what is it that we are asking? Before answering, it is useful to understand the foundation and motivating factors from which all ego-based decisions are made.

The ego is always fueled by fear, and the decision-making process of the ego runs off the same power source. The ego makes decisions based on fear and convinces us that these decisions are rational. More precisely, all ego decisions come from a fear-based thought system rooted in the following:

Fear of loss. I might lose something if I am not careful.

Fear of inadequacy. I may not be liked or approved of if I don't make the right decision.

Fear of time. I might waste time if I don't react properly and efficiently.

Fear of abandonment, based upon the fear of separation. I may offend someone and they will abandon me.

Fear of loss of power. Someone else might "get ahead" of me.

Fear of embarrassment, based upon feelings of shame. If I make the wrong decision it will prove that I am not worthwhile.

Fear of the body. I am physically unable to do what it takes.

Making decisions based upon fear allows the Ego Mind to convince us to make use of its finely honed skills—skills that actually reinforce fear. We begin to think that the ego's skills, which include judging, analyzing, comparing, critiquing, contrasting, avoiding, competing, and intimidating, result in making safe and secure decisions.

Yet decisions based on fear never result in our feeling safe and secure.

THE WHOLE MIND'S WAY OF MAKING DECISIONS

The Whole Mind approaches decision making from an entirely different angle than the ego; instead of fear, decisions are based upon trust.

What fuels the Whole Mind is quite different too. Peace of mind is the only goal the Whole Mind holds as valuable; all its decisions are based on the intention to create a tranquil mind.

Where peace of mind is my single goal, all
decisions become a reflection of my intention.

The following ideas are at the core of the Whole Mind's decision making:

> Giving and receiving are one in truth. Love cannot be lost. It can only be shared.

> Who I am is a whole, complete, and growing person. If I choose, all situations will teach me a lesson of love.

> The present moment always offers the choice: Do I want peace of mind, or do I want conflict?

> All minds are joined. In compassion for all life, the illusion of separation is overcome.

> True power comes from the ability to love ourselves and others unconditionally. To be powerful is to be unwavering in our commitment to peace of mind in all decisions that we make.

> Inner guidance, the quiet voice within, goes beyond all shame and whispers the truth. We need but choose to listen.

> My body and mind can work together. Nothing is impossible.

Though I still sometimes get trapped in the ego's way of making decisions, I have committed myself to learn the decision-making process of the Whole Mind. More specifically, as I allow myself to consistently practice quieting the endless chatter of the ego, the wisdom of the Whole Mind can begin to be heard.

A few years ago, I rented a guest house on our property to a woman and her daughter. Though I did not know them beforehand, our families became very close over a couple of years. One day she decided to move and gave thirty days' notice. Over a series of events, many aspects of our financial relationship became very confused, and we both had different beliefs about what was fair and equitable.

Anger entered our relationship. We both thought we were right. Both of us had a very difficult time accepting the other person's position. I was angry because I perceived that I was probably going to lose something: in this case, money. At the same time, I was also afraid of disapproval and feared losing the relationship. Though I was sure of my position, I was not as sure as I pretended to be. Sometimes when I feel insecure, I hide behind a facade of exaggerated confidence. To others this often appears intimidating.

All of this was a reflection of the Ego Mind's way of making decisions. Courtroom hallways are filled with people who were once friends and now fight one another. Fortunately, in this case, we decided somewhere along the way that there must be a better way.

I started by sharing more of how I was feeling on an emotional level. I told her how important she was to me and revealed all my fears. Most importantly, I began to shift my perception away from seeing us as wanting something different. I began to see our interest and goal as being one and the same: peace of mind. With peace of mind as my single goal, things began to shift from fear and conflict to love and joining.

Changing over to the the Whole Mind's way of thinking did not miraculously make all of my anger disappear. However, I was able to begin to share my feelings more constructively and appropriately. Three specific factors helped with this: I told myself to let go of the idea that someone had to be right and the other wrong; I was able to stop perceiving myself and the other person as separate and I began perceiving common interests and goals; and we both became more able to share exactly where we were without the fear of abandonment or judgment. I am happy to say that we are still friends, and we both see this experience as helping us to get beyond old ego-based habits. I will return to this story later in the book in a different context.

PASSIVE VS. CONSCIOUS DECISION MAKING

*Many passive decisions are characterized by
the statement "I have to."
Conscious decisions are characterized by
the statement "I choose to."*

In all circumstances, when we fear making a decision, there is a lack of trust. Because of this fear, many of us go through life without ever making clear and committed choices. We let other people make our decisions, form our opinions, and guide our lives. We become passive to the point where life seems to "just happen" to us. We seem to be just along for the ride.

Passive decisions are made without conscious or direct choice because we don't trust ourselves, our inner guidance, or God. I can't tell you how many couples I see who don't really know why they are together. They tell the all-too-common story of having come together for a period of time by choice, and then just continuing together. This is a passive choice because it lacks the deep feeling of love and compassion that comes with truly deciding to make a commitment to another human being.

Alan and Marie were a couple who came to me having never made any deeply conscious decision to be married. The pair had been married for nine years and had two children. Alan and Marie had dated each other for about six months when Marie became pregnant. They decided to get married primarily for this reason. They each felt that they "had to," not that they chose to. Both of them were good parents, but they lacked any sense of joy when they spoke of their children.

In our work together, my goal was not necessarily to keep them together. I wanted them to each come to a point where they could either *choose* to be in the relationship or consciously and responsibly choose to leave the relationship. In order to do this they had to work through and share their fears about both alternatives.

Alan was deeply afraid of being alone, and feared a life of great isolation if he chose to leave. He also feared committing to the relationship with Marie, because he was afraid of being controlled by her. He had grown up with a dominant and controlling mother. He told Marie of his secret fear that all women were really like his mother.

Marie feared committing to the relationship because Alan was fifteen years older than she was. She secretly feared that if she really committed to the relationship that when Alan died it would be unbearable for her. Conversely she feared leaving the relationship because she had been raised a Catholic. If she divorced Alan, she feared judgment from her family, the church, and God.

It is always an enriching experience for me to witness couples share their secret fears and come closer as they do. Alan and Marie spent about a year working with me and mutually decided that they wanted to commit to the relationship. Later, they created a ceremony for themselves and their children.

They all joined one summer evening at the ocean shore. Joining hands, they faced one another and spoke from their hearts. They spoke about who they were and what they wanted to offer the other family members. They made a conscious commitment to one another that truly transformed the passive family lives that they previously had.

Transforming passive decisions into conscious decisions allows a richness and depth to enter into our life. Changing "I have to" into "I choose to" can open up innumerable doorways in all areas of our lives.

THE CONFUSION OF PAIN AND JOY

When we choose to follow the ego's way of thinking and carry it to its logical conclusion, we will find ourselves totally confused about every aspect of our lives. It is not just the attitudes of the Ego Mind and the Whole Mind that we must identify and understand. The beliefs, or premises, that we choose will determine what we will accept into our mind. Therefore, we must also be able to see the end result of the ego's premise. By so doing, we may clearly sort out which thoughts are important for maintaining peace of mind and which kind always leave us with confusion and despair.

When I was twenty-one, a popular bar in my hometown offered me a job as an entrance manager—essentially a glorified bouncer. It was my task to determine at the door who was "appropriate" for entrance into the bar and who was not. When I made a mistake and let in a "troublemaker," it was then my task to tactfully and without incident remove that individual from the establishment. I knew that hiring me as a bouncer was a bit like hiring a rooster to guard a hen house, but I agreed to take the job.

My employment was short lived. Still, much later I realized that the experience taught me, metaphorically, something about dealing with my own mind. I like to think of my mind as an "establishment" that is committed to peace of mind. I have a "bouncer" at the door whose sole purpose is to determine whether a certain perception, thought, or belief is conducive to my peace of mind. If it is, I gladly let it in. If not, I send it on its way. Of course, there is the chance that the bouncer will make a mistake. In this case it is necessary to tactfully and without incident remove the "trouble-making thought" from my mind. The period of sorting out can be likened to a training period for your "bouncer." It is important to be able to determine what to let into your mind, and what to keep out.

Unfortunately, I have found that the Ego Mind also has its own type of bouncer. This bouncer is not really concerned with who or what comes through the door. It is more concerned with keeping our true nature hidden from our awareness. We may well know the Ego Mind's bouncer under another name: *denial*. Its purpose is to keep the awareness of love from us. The ego does not want us to see that we are whole and complete, because if we did, it would cease to have any power. One very important thought to grasp:

The Ego Mind may deny love, but it can't prevent
love from existing.

Our willingness to recognize or not recognize certain realities virtually has no effect on their existence. Let's take, for example, the existence of gravity. I cannot, as we know, *see* gravity. Yet if—based on my inability to see this force—I were to deny the existence of gravity, the physical reality of gravitational force itself would not, in any way, be altered. Indeed, it would still influence me.

The force of love is similar to the gravitational one: I may not *see* love, or even experience it, yet this has no effect on the fact that it is everywhere and is always available.

Trust, like love, is the logical outcome of the Whole Mind. Both exist whether we recognize them or not. A concept from *A Course in Miracles* recalls this fact in an eloquent way:

The ability to see a logical outcome depends on
the willingness to see it, but its truth has nothing to
do with your willingness.

During the period of sorting out, focus on gaining the willingness and desire to see the truth of who you are. Learn to listen to the Whole Mind by choice. During this period, you needn't concern yourself about whether what the Whole Mind tells you is true. You need only decide if you want to listen to it.

At this stage, you must begin to accept that you do not know the difference between what is painful and what is joyful, so that we may consciously choose between the two. Because at this point in the process of learning to trust, you are very likely inclined to confuse the two. Without a doubt, we all like to believe that at least we know what makes us happy, and the statement that we don't often meets with great resistance. Yet if we continue a little further, we may be surprised at how often this statement coincides with real experiences.

I personally have quite a long history of confusing pain and joy. From the time I was an adolescent, when I listened to the Ego Mind, I was told that I was incomplete, that I was full of guilt and shame, and that I needed something external to bring me joy. Consequently, I chose perhaps the most symbolic form of confusing pain and joy: drugs.

Initially, drugs seemed to bring me a sense of the joy for which I searched. In reality, they only took me farther away from the true joy of knowing myself through the perception of the Whole Mind. I began to believe that the only way I could experience intimacy, or joining, with another person was if I could get high and escape my awareness of self. The ego told me that if I looked within myself I would find despair and darkness. It professed that if I looked for joy outside of myself that I would find it.

All that can possibly result from such a belief is increased pain. I spent many years numbing my pain while thinking I was on the path to finding joy. Eventually, I arrived at a point where I truly felt that I either was going to die, or I was going to find a different way of being alive. Yet in terms of accomplishing the latter, I had no idea what to do or how to do it.

Eventually I stopped doing drugs, thinking that my pain would cease and joy would rush into my life right away. What happened was quite the opposite. All of the pain that I had been hiding came to the forefront. But this time it was different. I was in my twenties, and realized that what I had been doing had *caused* my pain. Joy was absent from my life. This simple realization provided the foundation for me to begin to change my life.

When we begin to examine our thoughts and beliefs, it is necessary and useful to continually remind ourselves of the obvious. Looking back at my own way of thinking, I had believed that doing the opposite of what the Whole Mind says was good for me. I needed to continually remind myself that this was not true. The best way I could remind myself of the obvious was to see the effects of my ego-based thinking.

> *The ego's wishes are meaningless,*
> *because the ego's wishes are based on the impossible:*
> *that fear is real and love is conditional.*
>
> *You can wish for the impossible.*
> *You can pretend that it is true.*
> *But this does not make it so.*
>
> *Love never abandons you.*
> *But you can pretend it does not exist.*

We are choosing to be weak as long as we avoid listening to the gentle guidance of the Whole Mind. Weakness brings on fear. Choosing weakness is choosing to perpetuate fear. And fear is at the core of the ego.

In the period of sorting out, we may feel that we are being asked to make sacrifices. It is important to know that the Whole Mind does not ask us to sacrifice anything. Sacrifice is a concept that belongs to the Ego Mind. When we become confused about this simple distinction, trust becomes impossible because we do not know which belief system to follow. Who would want to follow a guide that they didn't trust?

The ego uses fear to keep us from following the guidance of the Whole Mind. *Guidance becomes equated with fear.* And this leads to our having difficulty following any guidance at all. Such is the state of mind of many people. Having become so fearful and untrusting, a type of emotional and spiritual paralysis sets in. It is this paralysis that we must be willing to push through if we are to find what true joy is.

The Whole Mind is perfectly trustworthy. It is only through listening to fear that we continue to become confused—to the point that even pain and joy are confused. The way out of this confusion is to begin to trust that the voice of love will be there when we have the intent to listen to it.

In order to learn to differentiate between pain and joy, begin to practice following a specific premise or belief to its logical conclusion. Below is a list of life situations and related premises. Go through them, spending time thinking about the outcome of each one. Then write pain or joy at the end of each one. The answers may be rather obvious, but in developing trust it is important to point out the obvious answers to ourselves, and to constantly remind ourselves of their message.

1. My boss is being very unreasonable. I should be defensive and see him or her as the cause of my problems.

2. My spouse is distant from me today. In my mind I know that we are joined and I choose to be aware of how much I love him or her.

3. My parents were never really there for me. I should assume that nobody ever will be.

4. My friend lied to me about the money he needed to borrow. I see him as fearful and in need of love, not judgment and disgust.

5. My car won't start this morning. I know that my son used it last. I should be upset now and for the rest of the day. I should be very angry at my son when I see him.

6. My spouse has a problem. I can help my spouse without taking on his or her pain. I do not need to control them and their feel-ings. They are going through what they are going through for a reason. There are lessons to be learned.

7. I made a mistake. I look at it as an oppor-tunity to learn and have no shame about it. I know that I am a worthwhile person.

8. Joe did something different than the way I would have done it. I should tell him that he is wrong and should do it the right way, my way.

9. I was taken advantage of. One should always be on the lookout for bad people, and should never be vulnerable with anyone.
10. My spouse left me after ten years. I can't trust anyone.

The outcomes may seem obvious to you. Nonetheless, it is important to get in the habit of being able to treat every thought and belief that you have with the same attitude as you did in this exercise. Look at it and decide if it will lead to pain or joy. By doing so, you will be able to sort out what brings pain, and what results in joy.

STOP VALUING THE VALUELESS

If we hold onto what we previously attached value to (the ego's beliefs) we hinder our ability to transfer what can be learned in new situations.

Imagine that I wear glasses for nearsightedness and I obtain a new prescription because my vision has changed. Upon receiving my new glasses I still insist on wearing my old ones because I find them to be more comfortable and believe that they look better. It is obvious that even though I have what I need to see more clearly, I will not be able to do so until I choose to discard my old glasses.

The period of sorting out involves recognizing that we have a new way of seeing the world and ourselves. We have a new outlook which is trust-based instead of fear-based. Like a pair of old glasses we must throw the ego's beliefs away. Only then can we see clearly.

Because we are afraid to give up what we once valued, many of us try to keep the ego's way of seeing the world while we "try on" the Whole Mind's perceptions. This is synonymous with putting our new glasses on over our old glasses. We will still not see clearly.

Recognizing what is valuable and what is not requires us

to adopt an attitude of openness, unencumbered by the past. We can assess the value of everything based on whether it leads to peace of mind in the present moment. When we rely on the past to determine what is valuable in the present it is like trying to view a fine painting though a dirty glass window.

The present moment is the place where our perception is cleansed and we can see the value of love and trust. When its distorted view of the past is removed, the ego is like a toothless tiger; its roar becomes little more than humorous. Not seeing the past as valuable is how we make the statement, "I will no longer give value to shame, guilt, or judgment," a reality.

It is helpful to identify examples of what is valueless and what is valuable. The following list is not complete. Its purpose is merely to assist you in training your mind to more readily recognize what leads to conflict and fear, and what leads to peace of mind and trust.

THAT WHICH IS VALUELESS

- The more I have, the happier I will be.
  More money, more recognition, more
  material possessions; these are my goals
  above all else.
- The past is all important in determining my
  own and other people's self-worth. A "bad"
  past is a sure sign of a "bad" person.
- My body should be perfect in order for me
  to be happy.
- Getting old is bad.
- Loss is real because we are all separate from
  one another.
- What is valuable is that which makes me
  win, be better than, or have power over other
  people.
- Other people are responsible for how I feel.
  I am a victim.

THAT WHICH IS VALUABLE

- I have all that I need to have peace of mind in this moment. I am complete, and am abundantly full of love.
- In the present moment I recognize the value of every human being, including myself.
- Health is a state of mind. My happiness is only dependent upon my thoughts.
- We are each ageless. We are all teachers to one another, regardless of age.
- "Minds are joined." Matter (bodies, possessions, and so on) can disappear over time. Love, which is eternal, is unaffected by the passage of time.
- What is valuable is forgiveness. It allows me to join with another person.
- I am responsible for my feelings, my thoughts, and my actions.

In essence, the word "value" should only be accorded to that which is helpful in bringing about joining, trust, compassion, and love. This is not dependent on situational factors, but rather on our attitudes and beliefs. No matter what the situation, we can always be compassionate.

With this new perspective, it's easy to see that valuing the valueless leads to fear of loss and abandonment, feelings of isolation, and deep distrust. We must begin to train our minds to quickly recognize that whenever we are feeling any of these things we must examine the contents of our thought. Somewhere we are valuing something that has no value. We must begin to be willing to sort out everything in our lives simply on the basis of whether or not it has value. Until we do this we will see ourselves as victims of the world, caught in continuous fear.

EVERY SITUATION AND EXPERIENCE
IS NOTHING WITHOUT MEANING AND PURPOSE

How much easier our lives would be if we only recognized that everything is helpful in learning the lessons of love, and that nothing is devoid of meaning. Instead, many of us go through life fighting almost everything that happens to us. We often forget that there is potential for growth and learning in each situation.

When I speak to groups of people about this concept, someone in the audience will inevitably say: "How about Hitler and the death camps? These can hardly be seen as 'helpful' or 'meaningful.'" Though I would certainly agree that horrific situations exist in the world that are unjust and oppressive, there have also been people who have the courage and the ability to rise above these catastrophic situations, refusing to be limited by them.

The work of Dr. Victor Frankl has opened my eyes to the possibilities that the human mind has to transcend even the worst of atrocities of our time. Dr. Frankl, who survived the terror of Nazi concentration camps, recognizes that even in the most painful of circumstances one can find meaning. The existence of meaning is of fundamental importance, for it implies a decision to turn inward for answers to the deepest questions about what it is to be human. In an account of his experiences in several concentration camps, including Auschwitz, Frankl noted that even under such horribly adverse situations in which an individual has no control over his or her present circumstances, that individual can still determine what will become of him or herself, both *mentally* and *spiritually*.

In this sense, our destiny is not dependent upon the external world but rather upon our *perception* of that world. In the presence of death, and while enduring physical hardships beyond comprehension, Frankl and many others were able to find purpose and meaning in their lives. In his 1959 book, *Man's Search For Meaning,* Frankl eloquently and movingly described the power of love. In observing how he and his fellow prisoners found reason to live, he wrote:

> *[We saw] the truth—that love is the ultimate and the highest goal to which man can aspire . . . "The salvation of man is through love and in love."*

Frankl went on the describe how human beings can both create atrocities and transcend them:

> *After all, man is that being who has invented the gas chambers of Auschwitz; however, he is also that being who has entered those gas chambers upright, with the Lord's Prayer or the* Shema Yisrael *on his lips.*

The Ego Mind would have us believe that unless everything is exactly how *we* think it should be, we cannot be happy. The Ego Mind is in a constant battle of control. Nothing else is important to it. The Whole Mind sees the importance of acceptance. As a result of acceptance, meaning and purpose can unfold and take root.

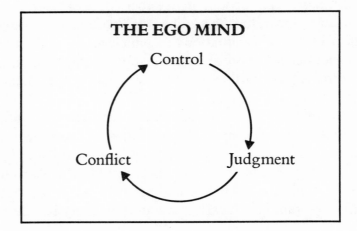

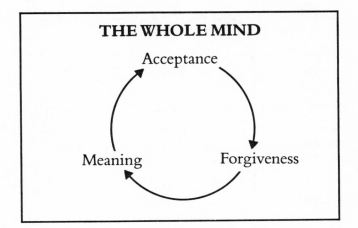

*There is no situation that has any power
whatsoever to take away your peace of mind.*

Let us today begin to remember that all situations—no matter how they appear—are opportunities to learn the lessons of love. There are not any circumstances that have any control over my peace of mind.

NO CHALLENGE,
NO RESISTANCE, NO INJURY:
A PHILOSOPHY

In the period of sorting out it is important for us to begin to think about our basic philosophy in life. It is difficult to sort out our lives if we don't first identify some of our basic ways of seeing the world.

There are certain aspects of the universe that, remarkably, hold much more than meets the eye—or even some imaginations. The black holes of the cosmos have time and light playing in dimensions that are beyond our usual perception of space and time. Holograms resemble sleight of hand magic to the child, yet they are real. Their two-dimensional images come alive and dance in a three-dimensional space that we can't see.

I believe that the teacher is often more important than the material being studied. In the Japanese martial art of Hakko-Ryu

Jujutsu and Seibukan Jujutsu, my teacher, Sensei Julio Toribio, has assisted me in exploring many facets of myself. In the course of this exploration, I have come to see how the three concepts of No Challenge, No Resistance, and No Injury occur naturally and simultaneously. As a black belt, these concepts continue to be my doorways to understanding the depth of trust, strength, and compassion. My understanding of them is only limited by my ability to set my ego aside and experience the essence of the universe.

Though I can speak of the three separately, their true meaning must be experienced together.

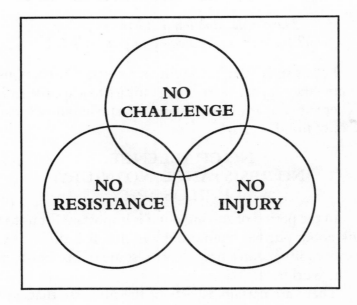

NO CHALLENGE

The many and varied aspects of life cannot be separated from one another. All that occurs in relation to our body, mind, and spirit is simply a microcosm of our life, and we can use this knowledge as a powerful tool. For example, when at the *dojo*, or martial arts school, I learn to avoid encouraging conflict with another student, it is far more likely that I may also be able to let go of a conflict when it arises in my home, on the streets, and in the world.

The philosophy of "No Challenge" also reflects the ability to see when my mind is using comparison as a means of determining self-worth. Comparison usually leads to either engaging in competition to "prove" superiority, or in withdrawing emotionally or physically and believing that I am inferior. Both originate in and reinforce low self-worth.

The concept of No Challenge recognizes the worth in each individual. From this stance, the individual may begin to join with others. Joining does not mean that I have to like someone's behavior, it simply means not seeing myself as superior or inferior. The ego only sees two modes: inferiority or superiority. In either, it is impossible to have peace of mind. In the past when I have thought that superiority would make me feel powerful, I was mistaken. Superiority only brings isolation and guardedness.

The ego deals in absolutes. I am either good or bad. I am right or wrong. I am either "better than" or "worse than." I am either liked by everybody or nobody likes me. I am smart or stupid. I am good looking or ugly.

When growing up in emotionally inconsistent or abusive homes, such as an alcoholic home, we come to believe that this polarized thinking will create safety for us. Because the ego deals in absolutes, we are either instigating or defensively and negatively responding to a challenge.

Not long ago a patient of mine was trying to make a career choice. She was extremely bright and very accomplished in her position as a scientist in a private research firm. The firm had a reputation for treating its employees poorly, and for this reason she was often on the defensive with respect to management. After a few years, her contract came up for renewal. She was very nervous about meeting with her bosses. She feared being challenged on all fronts, even though she knew in her heart she had been an outstanding employee. One day in my office she asked, "How can I possibly listen to what they say and not get defensive? To have any self-respect, I will surely need to fight back." The solution to this problem lies in the philosophy and practice of No Challenge.

In No Challenge, the emphasis is on knowing ourselves and trusting what we know. We do not need to become defensive. False accusations or provocation only have the power that we give to them. No Challenge says:

Know the truth, and respond only to it.
Don't see what is not there.

Furthermore, No Challenge incorporates the idea that our self-respect is not dependent upon defeating another. Nor is self-worth dependent on our making sure that everybody sees us as being right. The ego always sees the self as being threatened and in need of defense. The ego challenges others in order to validate itself. But the truth is, we ourselves need no defense because the self is love, and love needs no defense. The core of No Challenge is:

Love is who I am.
Love is lost in challenge.
Love needs no defense.

When we know this to be true, we trust ourselves. When we trust ourselves there is never any need to challenge another, nor is there ever any need to become defensive and attacking. With No Challenge we walk a peaceful path.

NO RESISTANCE

A blow with the force of a cannonball
becomes barely a pebble being tossed by a child.

Through practicing "No Resistance" we recognize and become sensitive to the intimate connectedness of all life. No

Resistance is applied in the same manner regardless if the aggressor is a verbal or a physical one. Many of us are taught, both directly and indirectly, that we should meet force with force. The phrase "take a punch" refers to the ability to emotionally or physically be able to "take" what is dished out. The problem with this is that sooner or later you can't "take" anymore. We either become hardened and distant, or shaky, fearful, and without any ability to assert ourselves. Force meeting force is not strength. It is an indication that we do not trust more subtle and gentle ways to respond to energy coming our way.

When we become *aware* of the subtle aspects of energy we can learn to yield rather than force. Force met with force creates very few choices. We simply lower our heads and plow through life. This approach to life leads inevitably to our becoming injured. Each time we become wounded our feelings of being unsafe increase. In turn, we build larger defenses. Contrary to the ego's thinking, *defenses always bring that which they were meant to guard against.* Thus when we meet force with force the following cycle occurs:

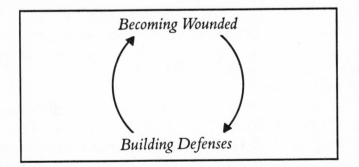

Becoming Wounded

Building Defenses

To create more options and choices in our life, learn the art of No Resistance. Once you yield to aggressive energy, then you may redirect that energy. You then have the ability to truly direct the exchange to a positive outcome.

In Hakko-Ryu and Seibukan Jujutsu there is a practice referred to as "henka." In henka, we are utilizing our intuition, or "dan," instead of our intellect. The intellect always pauses to assess and analyze the situation. Though the intellect has its place, responding to energy coming our way is not one of them. The intellect tends to respond in rigid, preconditioned ways. Intuition responds in fluid and creative ways through trusting our response to energy. Thinking and analyzing are absent. The result is a "dance" in which force is never meeting force.

This practice of henka helps to overcome resistance. It takes us beyond the intellect and opens up our intuition. If you truly allow intuition to respond, there will be no resistance. To the degree that we do not trust our intuition is to the degree that we meet force with force.

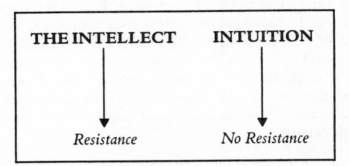

THE INTELLECT   INTUITION

Resistance   No Resistance

Resistance plays a key role in the process of psychotherapy. In fact, I feel that therapy can be seen as a process of working through our resistance. When we do so, resistance can be seen for what it truly is: fear.

Fear creates a lack of trust in ourselves, others, and the universe. At a certain point in my own therapy I was forced to see the effects of this fear. I had been dealing with the same issues, in the same intellectual place, for what seemed like years. I was trying to resolve issues with my parents. I wanted to sort out my feelings about them and my feelings about myself. The problem was that I wasn't feeling anything. I could talk endlessly "about" things, but I had great resistance to feeling. Then one day, with out any forethought, I trusted myself and my therapist enough to step aside and yield to the energy of my feelings. I laid back and began to cry. The sounds that began to leave my body were ones that I had never heard before. They came from deep within, from the center of my being. Sounds of pain filled the room, my whole universe. Time changed dimensions. I could have been there for a day or a minute; I wasn't sure. All of my hidden pain began to pour out in every sound. Tears finally found their way out of me in a genuine way.

As long as I was afraid of my pain I kept it hidden. It weighed me down in everything that I did. In my day-to-day activities, I was unaware of the energy I expended in order to keep my pain repressed. It was a process that drained me of vitality. Moving through my resistance opened up choices for me. Once I began to experience the pain I could then work through it. Forgiveness was then fully open to me. The love that had always been available to me filled my heart.

Willow in the wind
dancing in all directions,
yielding to each gust.

Waves upon ocean,
slowing, speeding, moving,
yielding to each current.

Fall to winter, spring to summer.
Changing, noticed but unnoticed,
yielding to each season.

May I learn from nature,
trusting my self,
yielding, choosing, loving.

NO INJURY

In absorbing the concept of "No Injury" we are finding a balance within ourselves. This balance allows us to move physically, emotionally, and spiritually, without becoming injured. It also teaches us how to not injure others. This balance is reflected in the following:

- Avoid violence and unnecessary confrontation.
- See kindness and strength as connected.
- Release the victim role.
- Become humble.
- Never attack, never defend. Take care of yourself while seeing the worth of others.
- Remember that hurting others is not a means of power.
- Strength comes from respecting ourselves and others, knowing ourselves, and being light on the planet.

As human beings, our basic survival depends on us individually and collectively adopting an attitude of No Injury. Yet the current global environmental crisis shows that we have taken another, more precarious path. We are ravaging the earth and depleting its resources. We injure the very air that we breathe, clear cut forests, and still somehow believe there will be no ill effect. Adhering to the principle of No Injury means understanding that cutting down an acre of rainforest in Brazil affects the entire planet.

Harming another human being, emotionally or physically, affects us in return. When was the last time that your making another person feel bad made you feel better in any lasting way? Our ego tells us that hurting another person can heal our pain. But upon closer examination, it is obvious that this behavior never gives us lasting peace of mind. Without the gentleness and compassion that comes with the adoption of No Injury, our species may not survive.

The present state of the world shows a desperate need for the adoption and practice of the philosophy of No Injury. In practical terms this means that if, for example, someone disagrees with me about an important issue, it would hardly be appropriate for me to take a gun and shoot them. It would be even more absurd for me to then go and shoot that person's entire family. The insanity of my decision would only increase if I were then to kill all of my adversary's neighbors. Yet this is the absurd logic behind the war mentality and weapons of mass destruction.

We must begin to adopt No Injury in our daily lives if we are ever to see it on the global front. Our safety is based on us changing our minds and our thoughts, not in developing weapons that can destroy us. Our society has become so used to thinking that injury brings us safety that we "normally" kill thousands of our fellow human-beings each year. This hardly makes for a safe home on the planet we share.

The ego injures because it seeks false strength through domination, judgment, control, and fear. The principle of No Injury means strength through open-mindedness, compassion, gentleness, and kindness.

No Challenge, No Resistance, No Injury.
Knowing Self, Trusting, Respecting.

CHAPTER FOUR

"The Period of Relinquishment"

From fear it is difficult to have an open heart.
It is through opening and releasing, not
closing and holding, that we learn
of love and trust.

The ego has done rather well at convincing us that our survival is dependent upon an insane thought system. Even after going through the period of undoing and the period of sorting out, the ego may still maintain a considerable hold on us. It propels itself by telling us the world is vindictive, harsh in all respects, and vengeful. There is a significant part of our thinking that still firmly believes that the way of the ego is our only protection.

In this chapter we are concerned with letting go of what no longer serves us. It is rare that this can be done without a certain amount of despair. For this reason this period calls upon and reinforces our faith, commitment to peace of mind, and courage.

RELINQUISHMENT:
THE TOOL FOR TRANSFORMATION

*We must begin to let go of what inhibits our
potential and happiness.*

Most of us grow up learning a set of values in direct opposition to the principle of relinquishment. We are taught that accumulating, acquiring, holding, and keeping are the hallmarks of success. We come to believe that learning is a process of filling our minds with information until no more will fit, and then packing just a little more in. We are taught that the past is very important and that being concerned about the future is very responsible. The problem with this kind of education is that there is little or no emphasis on the present moment.

True transformation—be it on a personal, interpersonal, or a global level—is only possible when we become willing to relinquish the values that are not conducive to achieving our goal: This is a difficult step because the ego tells us that we're nuts if we turn away from its platform of judgment, guilt, and acquiring.

*In order to forgive, we must be willing
to relinquish.*

In truth, once we relinquish the perceived "wrong doing," there is nothing left to forgive. In this respect, forgiveness and relinquishment can be seen as the same thing. If we see the period of relinquishment as a time of *giving up the desirable,* terrific conflict will be generated. Let's consider an analogy: Sometimes a baby cries when a toy is being taken away, even if that "toy" happened to be a sharp knife. In this same way, adults can also become quite upset when we think that we are giving up something that is valuable, even though it may be very harmful to us.

There is no point in sorting out the valuable from the valueless if the next logical step, relinquishment, is not taken. The simplicity of the Serenity Prayer illustrates the truth about relinquishment:

God, grant me the ability
to accept the things I cannot change,
the courage to change the things I can,
and the Wisdom to know the difference.

Relinquishment does not mean becoming a lump on a log, or not caring about the world and humanity. Nor does it mean developing an attitude of acceptance. Peace of mind requires that we relinquish all thoughts of wanting to change another person. We look upon them with what humanistic psychologist Carl Rogers termed *unconditional positive regard.* This means looking beyond the illusion of "badness," darkness, or negative self-image and towards the light of love that shines within us all. This leads to the ability to view ourselves in the same way. We must relinquish all the thoughts that we hold where we condemn ourselves for what we have done in the past. In other words, we must begin to let go of guilt if peace of mind is ever going to be possible.

THE FEAR OF LOOKING WITHIN

The Ego Mind builds a haunted house
full of ghosts, demons, and darkness in hopes that
we will never look within. When we do look within
it is as if the lights were turned on in a
carnival's haunted house. We then clearly see
the cardboard the demon is cut from,
and the wire attached to the ghost.
We laugh at what only a moment ago
seemed so real.

The fear of looking within ourselves is very common. Yet in my practice, I have witnessed countless courageous people confront and move beyond this fear. Listening to the Ego Mind, we become afraid to look within. We firmly believe that what we would find would be grotesque, beyond the possibility of healing.

Because of this we displace our guilt and shame onto others, unconsciously believing that we are getting rid of it.

The key word is *believe*. It is only our *belief* in shame and guilt that gives them any power. The Ego Mind thinks that it is quite appropriate to fear shame and guilt, whereas the Whole Mind sees them as only a scant veil covering the light of love.

The Whole Mind, which is true perception, never teaches us that we are shameful or guilty. When we finally decide to listen to the soft and gentle voice of the Whole Mind, we begin to relinquish fear. Deciding to look within, however, is a fearful thought to the mind that still listens to the ego, because we are afraid to see the ugliness that we believe is there.

In the Ego Mind, fear and shame fit together perfectly. For this reason we always seem to fear looking at our shame. The backbone of the ego-based existence is: "Have faith in shame and guilt, and be afraid to look at them." Loudly the ego shouts at us that we dare not look within. For if we do, the despair that we may feel will be so overwhelming we will not survive. Yet it is difficult to relinquish that which we will not look at. And so, through the use of fear, the Ego Mind stays intact.

The ego is most afraid of having us ask these questions:

- *What if there is really no shame at all?*
- *What if guilt is not there?*
- *What if I looked within and saw love and wholeness where I thought shame and fragmentation existed?*

Your simple interest in reading this book indicates you have already begun to question the thought system of the ego. And by contemplating the questions above, the ego begins to have less of a hold on you. You are starting to see that those who truly have peace of mind are those who no longer see their identity as tied to the ego. You are no longer entirely unwilling to look within. This is the most important step you will take in your personal development.

During the period of relinquishment, we take this partial liberation and make it more complete. We can begin to release the insane beliefs that the ego has told us are true. A window shade needs only to be lifted in order for the sun to come streaming through. Similarly, we only need to relinquish the guilt, fear, and shame that shadow our life for love to enter our lives. The result is trust, for trust is a facet of love.

By relinquishing, your faith turns inward towards the truth of who you truly are: love. You will know that you are immersed in the period of relinquishment when you fully realize the following to be true:

Personal freedom is when I am not afraid to look within myself.

DISPLACEMENT—THE OBSTACLE TO LOOKING WITHIN

Typically the Ego Mind sees the source of pain where it is not. When shame and guilt are believed to be enormous and without hope of being resolved, the mind finds ways to divert our attention from the true source of our pain. This is displacement. Unfortunately, the purpose of displacement is not to keep us "blind and happy," but rather is to keep us believing in the insane illusion that we are truly shameful and guilty. This can never lead to peace of mind.

Displacement is kept active by the belief that the source of guilt (to which attention is being diverted) must in fact be true. We become willing to see all kinds of *lesser* sources, as long as they are not the *deep* source. It is as if we were on a journey and, having asked a stranger for directions, were pointed in the opposite direction of where we wanted to go. Displacement points everywhere but to the area that needs to be relinquished. Most often these "lesser sources," furthermore, bear no relationship to the deeper one.

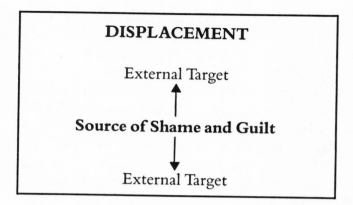

For quite a while in my personal relationships I was becoming a master at making the other person feel guilty. I irrationally believed that if I made another person feel guilty that it would lessen my load. In other words, I displaced my guilt (which I believed to be real) onto someone else, thinking that this would make me feel better.

I did the same thing with anger. I would invent things to be angry at. I would look for situations in which I could identify injustice, and then become angry. It was as if I had a pressure cooker of anger inside me, and I had to find some "justifiable" ways to let some of the steam off. And indeed, I would find great opportunities to get a lot of people to agree with me that I should be angry.

One such event took place many years ago. I was dating a woman who I was very serious about. I had future plans that involved our spending our lives together. I felt that I was "doing everything right" and that I was supportive to her in all ways that I could think of. Then we came upon a period where she was increasingly distant from me. We talked extensively about this and she assured me that she was simply going through a period of personal growth, and that everything would work out if I would be patient. It was about three weeks later that a friend divulged to me that she was having a relationship with another man.

I believed that I was "justified" in my anger and felt

that everybody would surely agree with me. Armed with self-righteousness, I became furious about the situation and confronted her with it. I was verbally abusive to her and my single goal was to make her feel guilty and ashamed.

The result was that we both felt a lot of things, but neither of us experienced any peace of mind. Even the most "justifiable anger" does not result in our experiencing peace. Eventually that relationship ended. It was not until years later, and many episodes of self-righteous anger, that I began to look to the deeper source of my anger, guilt, and shame.

What I found was that I felt unworthy of a positive relationship. I believed that many of the negative things that happened in my family of origin were my fault, and that I should have been able to fix them. When my parents would fight I would feel shame, even though their discord had nothing to do with me. For many years I was afraid to look at my shame. As a result displaced it onto others. This usually took the form of anger.

I have learned that the sources of our guilt and shame are nothing more than illusion. I believe that we are each guiltless, and created in the image of love. I have learned through experience that any time that I try to project my guilt on another person, the result will be that I will increase my guilt and inner conflict. The truth is:

> *If I see guilt in any relationship it is because*
> *I have put it there.*

If our guilt and shame are unexamined it is inevitable that we will displace them, seeing others as guilty. The main purpose of displacement is to perceive the source of guilt as being outside of ourselves and beyond our control. How can we relinquish that which lies beyond our grasp? Displacement chains us to guilt, and guilt chains us to the past. With displacement we cannot know love and we cannot understand what loving is. In other words, if we believe in guilt and fear, we will not believe in relinquishment and love.

I invite you to decide that you will no longer use any relationship to hold you to the past. You will not look within as long as you believe that your shame is real. You will not be able to relinquish your guilt as long as you believe that there is a reason for it.

The purpose of relinquishment is to dispel illusions, not to make them real and then let them go. In the period of relinquishment we learn that guilt and shame are products of the Ego Mind and are totally insane. The two daily lessons that follow help with this. The lessons help you in allowing each moment to bring a new awareness of love and trust.

INSTRUCTIONS FOR DAILY LESSONS

Beginning at this point in this book, you will periodically find daily lessons presented. The purpose of the lessons is to aid in the applied practice of the material that is presented. Theory is helpful, but alone it is insufficient: No one would want to have a doctor operate on them who had a theoretical foundation but no actual practice. It is highly recommended that you practice the lessons in the following manner:

1. Each morning, soon after rising, review the lesson for the day. Practice one lesson per day. It is important that you find a quiet place to practice, one where you won't be disturbed. Relax, and spend about five minutes reading the lesson slowly, keeping the lesson, which appears in boldface, in the forefront of your thoughts. During your practice time concentrate on the lesson and let any distracting thoughts go. If any unwanted thought interrupts your concentration simply acknowledge its presence and then let it go. During the day, as often as you can, slowly and thoughtfully repeat the lesson to yourself. This is especially useful in times of conflict.

2. Review the lesson periodically during the day for a few moments, preferably hourly. It is important that you apply the lesson to *all* people and *all* situations you encounter. Do not make exceptions. You may find it helpful to either carry the book with you, or to copy the lesson onto a 3 × 5 card.
3. In the evening, preferably right before retiring, take five minutes or more to review the lesson again. Think about your day and how the lesson applies to specific circumstances which may have been difficult for you.
4. When you have completed all of the lessons in this manner, it is beneficial to begin again and repeat the series. It is best to maintain this continual form of practice until you find yourself applying the lessons consistently in your life.

In brief, your daily practice consists of three parts:

1. *Your morning practice session.*
2. *An hourly review and application to specifics that arise during your day.*
3. *An evening review.*

LESSON ONE

"Above all else I want to see things differently."

This idea goes beyond surface goals. It begins to express a commitment to giving vision a priority in your life.

In order to see things differently you must relinquish the old way of seeing. You are probably living in a conflicted state of mind. But despite this discomfort, at this stage you may feel reluctant to practice the lesson with resolve because you still have attachment to the way that you see things *now.*

At this stage of developing trust, the purpose is simply to bring the idea a little closer than it was yesterday. If you find yourself tempted to think that this idea asks you to give up something that is desirable to you, remember this:

> *True vision has no costs to anyone.*
> *It will only lead me towards trust, love, and*
>   *compassion.*

I suggest that you repeat the lesson to yourself many times throughout the day. Remember that simply saying this phrase to yourself, especially in difficult situations, will help you to find a new way of viewing yourself and the world. How much you want this idea to be true will be reflected in how often you remember to repeat the phrase. Do not condemn yourself. If you find yourself forgetting and then remembering, thank yourself for reintroducing the idea, and then try to keep a more consistent schedule. Saying the lesson just once with sincerity will give you tremendous growth.

When applying the idea to material objects it can feel a little silly. Saying, "Above all else I want to see this table differently," for example, sounds almost comical. How we "see" an individual chair hardly seems to have a great affect on our life. But this deserves closer examination. We need *to be willing* to see anything our eyes rest on in a different way. To allow a "newness" into our lives we must be willing to relinquish our "old" way of seeing. In this regard, just being willing to see a table or a chair differently is a useful exercise in opening our mind to the present moment, unencumbered by the past. In so doing, we begin to see the aspects of our world as connected by a genuine unity. As we begin to acquire "present vision" we see more clearly the intimate connections of all aspects of life.

When we say, "Above all else I want to see clearly," we are committing ourselves to relinquishing our preconceived ideas from what we are viewing. We are opening our minds to what is in front of us. We cease to define ourselves by what occurred in the past. There is a distinctively different experience when we turn within and ask what something—or someone—is instead of *telling* it what it is.

Creativity is directly related to this concept. For example, if I bind the meaning of the chair to my limited experience of chairs, I will probably miss many creative opportunities that someone else may see. The artist may notice its unique form. The wood worker may become fascinated by the subtle patterns of the wood grain. The child may become excited at the potential of making it a jungle gym or a foundation for a fort. Creativity is a direct result of relinquishment and open-mindedness.

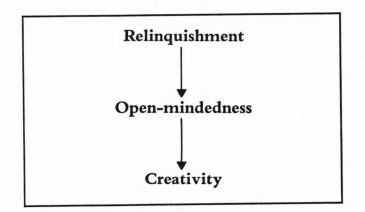

Creativity is also important in relationships. Many times we assume we "know all" about someone instead of seeing the person in light of the present moment. *The greatest mistake that I can ever make is thinking that because I have past experience of someone that this means that I know all of who they are.* Think about the absurdity of this thought. Even if I spent my whole life with a person, that says nothing about their capacity for growth, transformation, depth, and potential in the moment. Just as an astronomer would never look through a telescope and say, "I know the universe and all that lies beyond," let us never look at another human being and think that we fully know the depth of who they are.

Today commit yourself to not limiting your vision. Release your past ideas. Look on everything and everybody, including yourself, with newness and a creative spirit.

LESSON TWO

"All fear is past and only love is here."

This lesson is designed to aid you in beginning to relinquish your negative thoughts, judgment, guilt, and shame. The result of this process is forgiveness.

When the source of the fear is gone, all fear becomes a thing of the past. Fear-based thoughts disappear with it. With the absence of fear, love is free to be itself. It is impossible for the world to be a safe and joyous place as long as we hold on to all of our past mistakes, as if they were cemented into our very being. Relinquishment creates the ability to focus on the present moment rather than being chained to the past. Love and trust become our companions where fear and distrust once stood.

Relinquishment can serve us every time we have a negative judgement about ourselves or another person. As we become more willing to let go of these thoughts, we are less affected by the ego's ranting and raving. At times, it may still deceive us, but it will do so only in increasingly shorter periods. Most of us are a long way from being able to say that we never harbor negative thoughts or participate in conflicts in our relationships. Progress needs to be measured, first, by how willing we are to recognize what we are doing, and second, by how willing we are to let it go and ask for a different perception of the situation. More specifically, anytime that we are not experiencing peace of mind, we need to go through the following three steps:

1. Ask yourself: "What thoughts am I having right now that are shame-based, are negative

judgments, or come from feelings of inadequacy?" Examples: "She is a terrible
person for not arriving on time." "I am
worthless for not being able to do a particular job better." "I can't succeed at this."

2. Tell yourself: "This is untrue and is based
on fear." Picture a giant stop sign in your
mind, illustrating that you want to stop
this thinking. Then picture a garbage can
into which you put this thought, releasing
it from your mind.

3. Ask your Whole Mind for a different
perception: Examples: "Her tardiness gives
me an opportunity to spend time with
myself." "My abilities are not reflective of
my worth." "Many of my limitations are
self-imposed."

Look gently upon yourself and others.
Follow your faith in love.
Be not deceived or bound by the insane insistence
of the ego proclaiming your shame and guilt.

Through relinquishment the quiet and peaceful path
is now open to you. Follow it joyfully.

THE IMPOSTER SYNDROME

It is surprising how tenaciously negative thoughts mani-
fest themselves in and attack even the most "successful" people.
One such manifestation of non-relinquishment is the "Imposter
Syndrome."

We can define this syndrome as a collection of feelings
of inadequacy that stem from the belief that one is insufficient
as a person, and unable to be proficient at an activity that individual wants or needs to do. These feelings persist even when all

information that he or she receives indicate that the opposite is true. The following describes two different examples of the Imposter Syndrome.

Both sides of my family have done well in terms of social and monetary success. My father and his brothers became doctors; my mother is a well-known designer. In the eyes of my relatives, there seemed to be little doubt that I would "amount to something." My parents gave me a lot of positive support, however, the fact that I also received many mixed messages was much less evident. Our family always appeared "in good shape" from an outside perspective, but internally there was a great deal of tension. I felt deeply affected by the many arguments that occurred, and by the alcoholism that went on within our home.

It was not that our family was devoid of love—I knew that family members cared about me. Yet I did feel that external images and internal feelings were never to be the same.

As predicted, I began to do well in life, in some cases overachieving, yet I always felt that I was not deserving of anything I received. Particular experiences in my life seemed to drive this point home. I grew up with horses and was on the horse show circuit at an early age. When I was about thirteen I remember a certain show in which I won every event that I was in. Even though I was winning, I still felt that there must be some kind of mistake. I didn't really believe that I could be good at anything. I felt that I was an imposter.

When my picture appeared in a small newspaper for my achievements I began to feel that maybe I was worthy and actually good at something. About three weeks later I had a shock that confirmed all of my original suspicions. I overheard a conversation between my horse trainer and the man who was the judge at the horse show where I had won so much. It appeared that my winning was, at least in part, an arranged event.

For many years after that, no matter what I was doing, I felt that I was an imposter. When people liked me, I thought that if they really knew me and all of my thoughts, they would reject me.

This cycle continued to occur all through college. Although I ended up with a very high grade point average, I felt as though I were not intelligent; rather, I felt as though I were a person who came without all the required pieces. I believed that I constantly had to "fake it" to show that I was worthy and whole.

I used drugs to numb my feelings. This only led to a vicious cycle. I felt that no matter what I was doing well, the fact that I was using drugs proved that I was worthless. My feeling of worthlessness in turn made me increase my use of drugs. It was not until I decided to finally look within and entered therapy that, at last, I began to see that I was not deficient in some area. I found that I could actually have my inner feelings be safely reflected in my external image.

In the process of realizing my wholeness I have had to constantly watch my ego-based thinking. For me, when the ego's beliefs surface, I have made relinquishing these thoughts my highest priority. In doing so I have found what I had inside me all along: self-respect and love.

Sometimes I still become caught up in the cycle of feeling like an imposter. Writing books I sometimes feel that I don't practice what I preach: If people really knew me, I would probably be denounced as a fraud. When I think this I remind myself to keep in mind the thought most important to peace of mind: that it is my intention to teach what it is I want to learn. I do not have to be perfect all of the time. I try to remind myself that "I am whole, and I have nothing to fear." I have found that the best way to reverse feeling like an imposter is to:

- *Trust that peace of mind is possible in every situation.*
- *Trust that revealing myself is safe because beneath all that I feel is "not good" lies perfect and undisturbed love.*
- *Relinquish all value that I have placed in the Ego Mind.*

Some years ago, a young man named Al came to see me in my practice. Al was eighteen years old when he came to therapy. He was raised by two very bright parents, who were quite successful in their careers. The father had been a professional athlete, and later became involved in the computer industry. There was a strong nonverbal message that Al would excel in sports and in academia. At the age of eight, Al was found to have a moderate learning disability that made it very difficult for him to excel scholastically. Athletics became his haven, his sanctuary of excellence.

When Al first came to see me he had just received a full baseball scholarship to a major East Coast university. He was terrified of going, and was, in fact, thinking about turning the offer down. When I asked him what his worst fear about going was, he responded: "I have nightmares that I am pitching in a game. I am on the mound and everything goes to pot. I can't get the ball anywhere near the plate. Then everybody in the stands begins to shake their heads disapprovingly. When I look closer, I see my father in the stands with his back to me. Everybody finally knows that I'm really no good."

With the Imposter Syndrome this type of fear, and even nightmares, are very common. The core fear is that one will be found out to be a fraud, a fake. Inadequacy will finally, in one fell swoop, be seen by all.

I worked with Al both individually and with his family. Al finally was able to give himself permission to ask questions of himself that he had never asked before. He was able to ask himself if he truly liked playing baseball. He began to see that he did have an identity beyond the pitcher's mound. He had never allowed himself to see it before because he felt that he was inadequate in everything. Baseball had become little more than a good place to hide. Al's nightmare reflected that he feared being stripped of his one hiding place, and that all of his insecurities would show.

As Al was able to explore his inner world, he realized that he always felt inferior to his father. No matter how well he did he still felt that sooner or later he would be found to be not good enough. He also realized that almost all of his life had been devoted to pleasing his father and hiding his insecurities. Al was able to make his own life choices for what *he* wanted. He was able to feel more responsible for his life. The cycle of the Imposter Syndrome gave way to a more whole and healthy existence.

Al ended up doing quite well in college. He truly *chose* to play baseball. For the first time his life became his own. It was pure joy for me when, last summer, I saw Al and his father playing catch on the beach in Carmel. They were actually *playing* together. The pleasure in their motions indicated to me that, for Al, competition and performance were a thing of the past.

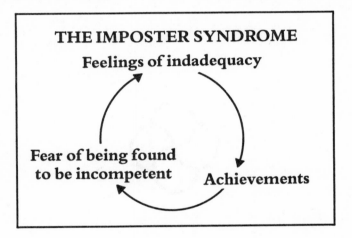

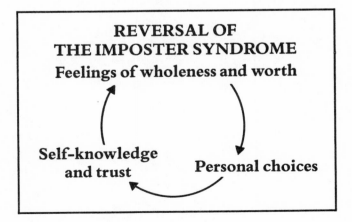

CHAPTER FIVE

"The Period of Settling Down"

It is as if we have been at sea in a severe winter storm, in a boat that has lost its rudder. Finally the sun breaks through, the waves die down, and land is spotted. We have a long-awaited period of settling down.

When we commit ourselves to a life in which we consistently practice relinquishment, we eventually begin to feel the positive effects of our efforts. When we are willing to relinquish the thought system of the Ego Mind, there is no context in which we cannot experience peace of mind. With this knowledge comes a sense of calm.

CONSOLIDATING OUR LEARNING

Many of us have become so used to working on ourselves, our personal growth, and our relationships that we sometimes end up thinking that if we are not struggling with these issues, something is wrong. We become suspicious of any quiet or calm in our lives. In the development of trust there are two periods in which we feel a sense of tranquility and calm: "The period of settling down" is the first. We need to be vigilant, though, because it is also easy to mistake this period for the end of our journey, to become complacent in our inner work.

83

In psychotherapy, I see people approach this period of settling down in one of two ways. They may begin to question our work and wonder if another form of therapy or therapist is needed. In the earlier periods of developing trust, there is a great deal of activity and inner exploration. In the period of settling down, there is more of a consolidation of learning. If this is not understood, one may decide to leave therapy (or whatever growth work they may be doing) in order to become "stirred up" again. Odd as it may seem, many people have to have some crisis in their lives to feel "secure."

Another group is made up of individuals who have been waiting for the day that they "find all the answers." They dislike any kind of internal struggle. When they at last feel the struggle subside, they are convinced that they have completed their inner journey. This is only complicated by the eventual letdown of finding that their peace of mind has not yet been firmly established. They become quite disillusioned when the next period unsettles them. The important thing to remember is that this is a period of consolidation. It is time to implement what we have learned thus far, and then move forward.

SEARCHING AND FINDING

The Ego Mind is certain that unconditional love is dangerous. Its primary goal is to teach us this. But the ego has another, hidden lesson to teach, a basic tenet that it does not reveal to us: "Seek but do not find." When following the guidance of the ego, one seeks peace of mind but never finds it. When we believe that the ego's thought system is valid, we find ourselves obsessively in search of love.

Any search that the ego undertakes ends in defeat. Thus, when we are following the voice of the ego, which is telling us that we are somehow incomplete and must "find" love, we always end up feeling defeated by ourselves. Indeed, self-defeat and following the ego's course go hand and hand. A quote from *A Course in Miracles* summarizes:

...the ego cannot love, and in its frantic search
for love it is seeking what it is afraid to find.

We can begin to see the ego for what it is as our trust in love becomes more firmly rooted in our lives.

PERFORMANCE-BASED VS. PRESENCE-BASED APPROACHES TO LIFE

During childhood, many of us learned that conditional love was the only love in existence. Parents can sometimes unwittingly teach children that love has to do with performance rather than being.

Performance-based child rearing teaches that if the child meets certain expectations he or she will be deserving of love. The child hears a covert message that "being loved is based upon satisfying another person's expectations and desires." A performance-based approach to self leads only to fear and an endless pursuit for acceptance and approval from others. When we follow this approach to self, we search endlessly for love but never recognize love within ourselves.

Conversely, presence-based (or "being-based") child-rearing teaches that love is who we are, and we are all lovable. Here, a person's self-worth is not dependent upon accomplishments or achieving some externally prescribed goal. During the period of settling down we begin to learn that a presence-based approach to who we are leads to feelings of calm and self-esteem. For the development of trust, it is imperative that we understand the difference between performance-based and presence-based approaches to self. Until we do, we only continue to distort love. In a performance-based approach, the ego sets us on a journey that can only lead to futility, hopelessness, and despair.

How can we develop trust in such a predicament? To seek and not find is certainly not joyous, and most certainly is not conducive to developing trust. When we turn inward and adopt a presence-based approach we will create the opportunity to recognize love. Self-defeat is gently transformed into self-esteem. The roots of self-esteem are in the knowledge that we are lovable. With self-esteem, we do not need to seek outside ourselves any longer.

Up until today, you may have been following the irrational guidance of the ego because you knew no other way. You may not remember how to look within for the simple reason that you don't believe your home is there. Yet there is a part of you that does remember, and that part will faithfully guide you towards love. All that is needed is a little willingness to turn away from the ego, and towards the heart. It is only your mind that believes in the ego and accords reality to it. Yet it is also your mind that can choose to turn away from it and towards love. Now all our attention is focused on doing this.

Much of my life I thought that there was an emotional price to pay for love. I believed that either I had to do something or sacrifice something in order to experience love. I spent much of my time either chasing after accomplishments or denying a part of myself in order to be accepted. I did not feel lovable. I believed that I had to "buy" love. Even when I was receiving love and acceptance, I was still secretly convinced that if I was not achieving I would not be loved.

Slowly I have learned that I was mistaken. I have come to know that love is neither bought nor sold, it is simply recognized or denied. With the consistent help of others, I have found that who I am at this moment is the most important decision that I can make. If I decide that I am full of darkness and guilt because of the past, I will not find love. I will certainly not trust myself, others, or my environment. Conversely, if I decide that I am whole and worthy of love, acceptance and love will be my experience. The recognition of love is something that we decide upon every minute of every day. And it is always dependent upon our belief of who we are.

A QUIET TIME

The period of settling down gradually brings peace from internal conflict. One of the main problems that presents itself in this period is that we are simply *unaccustomed* to having a calm and quiet mind. We may actually be a bit *uncomfortable* with tranquility. We don't trust it. We may even be bored. We have become so used to a split and conflicted mind that anything else seems abnormal.

In this period, we must treat our tranquility as though it were a beautiful estate for which we are the caretaker. Anytime weeds or unwanted intrusions present themselves, we must be quick to deal with them in order to maintain our tranquility.

As I have described, even when things are going well in our life, we can feel very uncomfortable. This was the case for Sam, a man who never quite felt safe in his life, no matter what the circumstances. If things were not going well he worried ceaselessly. If things were going wonderfully he wondered when something was going to go wrong. Because of all of the things that had gone wrong in his life he became very preoccupied with external events and trying to predict the future. He did not trust peace of mind when it did arrive.

Sam worked extremely hard on his own personal growth to finally experience a sense of tranquility. He became understandably frustrated when he couldn't enjoy the feeling, because he was worried that something would happen to take it away. By adopting a daily practice of quieting his mind, he finally became comfortable with his inner peace. He saw that peace of mind was not dependent upon all of the external events that he worried so about.

At first, Sam's tranquility was like a land that he had been forbidden to enter. He had always believed in the logic of the ego: "Beware at all times, only a fool would let his guard down." Yet, as Sam discovered that his tranquility was the safest place for him to be, he found that no situation had the power to take away his calm state of mind.

Although our interpersonal relationships are an important area to focus upon in the course of developing trust, it is also important that we spend time alone. Indeed, with our busy schedules, some of us spend very little time alone at all. And even when we do, it is often task-oriented—commuting to work, cleaning the house.

In our society today we have books, movies, and endless entertainment options. We are often quick to fill free time with some form of amusement. Though many of these are certainly useful (in that they are creative expressions), they can also distract us from our *inner* journey.

The statistics on the number of hours that the average American watches television are staggering. We seem to have become used to giving in to a constant need to be entertained—to be taken away from ourselves. We have become fearful of being alone, afraid to be without somebody who we can call "our" spouse, friend, and so on. In short, we become afraid to be with ourselves without any distraction. This is the way of the ego: It convinces us that we should be afraid of what is inside ourselves in order to keep us searching outside ourselves.

To develop trust we must commit to spending time with ourselves: a walk in the woods, contemplative time in the morning, watching the waves on the beach. We must be willing to begin to observe the subjective happenings within ourselves.

Have you noticed how lonely so many people are? Have you noticed how when you try to be alone with yourself, away from distractions, that you quickly want to escape from yourself and what you are? All of this is because we have become afraid of who we are.

BOREDOM

What is boredom? We rarely look into what boredom really is because we are so busy running from it. Much of what people fear most is boredom. Indeed one of our society's most lucrative industries, the multibillion-dollar entertainment business, is primarily geared toward relieving our boredom.

To find true contentment we must be willing to examine and explore the roots of our boredom. Simply put, boredom is caused by loneliness. The philosopher J. Krishnamurti expresses this most eloquently:

> *If you inquire a little into boredom you will find that the cause of it is loneliness. It is in order to escape from loneliness that we want to be together, we want to be entertained, to have distractions of every kind: gurus, religious ceremonies, prayers, or the latest novels. Being inwardly lonely we become mere spectators in life; and we can be the players only when we understand loneliness and go beyond it.*

In spending time with another person, there are two very different kinds of being "together." In the first, we are together because we are afraid to be alone. In the second, we are together because we want to fully share ourselves while also coming to know the other person. When we are together because we are afraid to be alone, we are living a very tragic life; essentially, out of fear, we come together because we want a distraction from our boredom and loneliness. Authentic love is very difficult to discover in such a relationship.

Most of us do not really know how to live alone. It is a paradox that we really must be able to live alone in order to effectively live together. Before we can truly have close and intimate relationships we must be able to move through our fear of being alone. If we don't move through this fear—and most do not—then our life becomes an endless pursuit for distractions from loneliness.

To work through your aloneness, we don't have to leave the relationship in which we may now be involved. It is the willingness to confront, explore, and work through our *internal* aloneness that is important. Beyond loneliness lies the greatest (and often least expected) gift that we can discover: knowing that we are loved and whole.

In the early 1980s I became involved in groups that used wilderness experiences to pursue personal growth. My main interest in this came after I experienced a Native American ritual called a Vision Quest. The term Vision Quest suggests that the purpose of the experience is to seek guidance in life through a profound spiritual experience. My experience consisted of ten days in the wilderness, three days and nights of which were spent alone.

During the three days and nights that I was alone, all that I had was water and a tarp, nothing else. I had no distractions to which I could turn. The previous several days were devoted to various rituals and meditations geared towards letting go of my attachments to people and possessions. I was able to meet myself and confront my loneliness. The resulting experience was profound for me, and I became more interested in helping to create this experience for young people.

In our society, young people are met with a blitz of distractions. Some distractions, such as schoolwork, are seen as culturally valuable. Others, such as drugs, are considered valueless. Our society provides very little, if any, time and support for youths to find and explore themselves. A a result, we have rising gang violence and drug use, as well as many "lost souls."

It is time that we begin to create a culture that values and respects self-knowledge rather than one that devotes itself to fighting and running from aloneness and boredom. The place to begin is within ourselves. With self-knowledge and understanding we can truly be of service to others, because we then have something important to give: love and compassion. Demonstrating the value of knowing ourselves and being of loving service also creates healthy role models for our youth.

LEAD-FEELINGS
AND CORE BELIEFS

During the period of settling down we begin to be more aware of all aspects of ourselves. In particular, our feelings become more available to us because we do not have the thoughts and distractions that previously kept us from experiencing them. For it is difficult to experience the full range of our feelings when we are full of fear and have no trust or faith. Our mind becomes full of worry and dread.

In many personal-growth experiences, such as psychotherapy sessions, groups, or retreats, a great emphasis is put on what the individual is feeling. I agree with this emphasis in part. Yet so often, when we are asked, "What are you feeling?" the question might as well be, "What does the other side of Mars look like?" Many of us are so out of touch with our feelings that we do not even know where to start in our search for our inner experiences.

A "lead-feeling" results from a specific belief. It affects all other facets of our inner life. For years I harbored a core belief that if I became too close and vulnerable to another person, I would be swallowed up and would lose myself. This belief stemmed from experiences I had in my family of origin. As a child, at times I felt smothered emotionally by other people. Other times I felt responsible for relieving their emotional pain. Yet I was ultimately unsuccessful in making everyone feel all right and the resulting feeling—the lead-feeling—was one of shame and inadequacy. Because of my "core belief," and the resulting lead-feeling of shame, all other experiences were in some way permeated with shame.

Our ego tells us that certain feelings, such as shame and fear, are not just feelings, but are *who we are*. During those years when I experienced shame, it did not feel like a transitory feeling. I believed that *who I was* was shameful. With a belief such as this, who would want to experience any more feelings? When shame is at the core of who we believe we are, any experience of any feeling increases our sense of shame. By adulthood I became so guarded and distant that I was rarely able to access what I was feeling at any specific time.

Lead-feelings are based on core beliefs. They reinforce each other, thus greatly influencing our life.

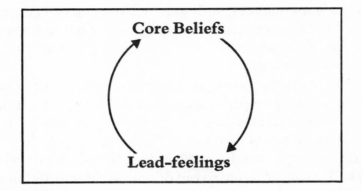

Fortunately lead-feelings can also be positive. I am continuing to learn that I no longer have to be smothered if I become close to another person. I also know that we are each responsible for our own feelings and experiences. As I choose to adopt these new beliefs I begin to have more of an openness to love.

Love is also a lead-feeling. Love will permeate all areas of our life if we begin to move away from the thought system of the Ego Mind.

Because our core beliefs determine lead-feelings, it is extremely important to address our beliefs. Up until the period of settling down, this has been our task. Now we can begin to focus on the feelings that we have been afraid of in the past.

As you look at and experience your feelings I encourage you not to be analytical or critical. You may be tempted to say, "Oh, I shouldn't feel this." Allow yourself to experience your feelings as though you were taking a walk in a forest that you had never been in before—full of plants that you had never seen. Take joy in each feeling that comes into your awareness.

If you find yourself feeling consistently uncomfortable, pause for a moment: Your belief about what you are feeling may be causing the discomfort. Therefore it would not be the feeling that needed to be stopped, but rather the belief examined. Let's take an example. Suppose that you have been shut off from your feelings for quite some time. You begin to feel some anger towards your father for not having been around much while you were young. You begin to feel guilty about feeling angry and want to stop or repress the anger. Yet upon closer examination, you find that the guilt is not caused by the fact that you are angry. The guilt stems from the fact that you *believe that it is bad to feel anger* towards your parent. To proceed, you must begin to allow all of your feelings and thoughts to be experienced. We cannot release that which we continue to repress.

Below are some more examples of thoughts that produce lead-feelings of shame, and then thoughts that produce lead-feelings of love. A good rule of thumb is this: Any thoughts that create separation lead to fear; any thoughts that create joining lead to love. Remember, when you experience fear-based feelings, you shut yourself off from the rest of your feelings. As a result you feel unsafe in your environment. In contrast, when you experience love-based feelings, you always welcome and trust the rest of your feelings. This creates feelings of safety.

True security is not fearing any aspect of yourself.

BELIEFS THAT PRODUCE LEAD-FEELINGS OF SHAME, FEAR, AND GUILT

1. It is better to be quiet and always be sure that everybody is happy.
2. Men should never show emotion because it is a sign of weakness.
3. Women should always be "agreers" and "peacekeepers."
4. My negative childhood can never be overcome.
5. I don't remember anything about my childhood. If I begin to remember I will be overcome with negative feelings and won't survive.
6. Other people are responsible for how I feel.
7. My body is bad and my sexual feelings are shameful.
8. Anything new or different automatically means failure.
9. What I feel is wrong. Expressing my feelings is bad.
10. I am not worthy of your love. I should be suspect of it.

BELIEFS THAT PRODUCE
LEAD-FEELINGS OF LOVE

1. It is okay for me to have an opinion. Every-body does not have to approve of me.
2. What I feel is all right. Fully experiencing a feeling and being weak have nothing to do with one another.
3. Disagreements do not mean anything about me or the other person. My goal is still joining, even in disagreements.
4. There is nothing that can't be overcome through forgiveness.
5. We have to bring up feelings and memories in order to let them go.
6. We are each responsible for how we feel.
7. Unity of body and mind comes as we accept ourselves and care for our body.
8. New and different situations present themselves as opportunities to learn.
9. What I feel is acceptable. It is important for me to express what I feel.
10. Love knows no limits. We are all worthy of love.

CHAPTER SIX

"The Period of Unsettling" and "The Period of Achievement"

Although we have now experienced the major periods or stages in developing trust, we have not yet achieved consistent peace of mind. Indeed, just at the moment when we think we have worked through all of our conflicts, anger, and guilt, the period of unsettling saunters in like an unwelcome guest. Indeed, we come to realize that we do not really know all that we thought we knew about ourselves. Even after spending a considerable amount of time sorting out our beliefs and relinquishing those we have no use for, we must see that we still do not really know what is valuable and what is valueless.

All that has been learned so far, during the course of the previous periods, is that we do not want the valueless and that we do want the valuable. The goal of the newest step, the period of unsettling, is to set all personal judgment and evaluation aside and to turn inward and ask what we really want.

This can take quite some time and will be difficult if all of the other steps were not firmly established. Difficulty vanishes when we refuse to view any experience as sacrificial. In learning to ask for inner guidance it is imperative that we understand the difference between sacrifice and choice.

SACRIFICE VS. CHOICE

The Ego Mind tells us that we should accumulate, hold on to, win, collect, and do anything else that will result in us "having more." To the ego, the idea of "letting something go" is completely insane. Yet the ego recognizes that sometimes we do things that we don't want to do. Because of this the ego created the process of sacrifice. This process goes something like this:

You ask me to do something or give up something that I wouldn't do unless you requested it of me. I go ahead and do what you request. But I believe that I am *sacrificing* because I am doing this only for you. I am thus *losing* something. Because of my sacrifice I can expect you to be indebted to me, or at a minimum, to shower me with thanks. If you do not do what I expect in return, I then have every right to be resentful and angry at you. I will say things like, "After all that I have done for you," or "I have given you the best years of my life."

As long as you believe in the idea of sacrifice, your mind will be clouded. It will be impossible for you to experience the benefits of releasing beliefs and values that you don't want. The Ego Mind hordes, whereas the Whole Mind releases.

The idea of sacrifice is foreign to the Whole Mind. In the Whole Mind, all decisions and choices are made from turning inward and asking for guidance. As long as we have the courage to listen and follow what we hear, we will find peace of mind through personal responsibility.

Taking responsibility means that what we do we *choose* to do. We have confidence that what we are doing is exactly what we are supposed to be doing. This includes accepting responsibility for the consequences of our choices—a subject that deserves a little more discussion.

Many of us make decisions based upon what the consequences of our decision might be. If we like the consequences we do it. If not, we don't. This sounds quite logical to the Ego Mind.

The guidance that we receive when we turn inward and ask does not always lead to consequences that we would like to choose for ourselves. Also, when we ask for guidance from within, we often do not readily understand the answer that we receive. This answer might sound crazy, or the consequences might seem severe.

At the time of this writing, the Persian Gulf War has been underway for about one week. I have had many feelings come up over the last week, including my share of sadness, despair, and outrage. Many of the people that I have spoken with have also been in this "stirred up" state. Recently, I was talking to a friend, Julio, who had served in one of the elite forces of the military when he was a younger man. He had become very accomplished at attack and defense. Since his period of service in the army, Julio has done a great deal of work on developing himself personally. He let go of a great deal of anger and exaggerated male behavior and attitudes. He found that throughout much of his life he had carried a great deal of shame and has masked it by being able to overpower and dominate others. In the years since he left the service, Julio worked through much of his shame and no longer felt the need to be dominant and controlling. He found a new softness and gentleness within him that beams across the room when he speaks. The problem that he confronted with respect to the present war situation is that, through the reserves, he still owed the Army two years of service. War looked imminent, and although he had not yet been called up, the likelihood loomed over him.

In our conversation during the last few weeks, it seemed that Julio was very confused about what to do. On the one hand he did not want to be involved in combat and killing. On the other hand, he knew that he had made a commitment, and he did not take this lightly. The consequences of not going would either mean looking over his shoulder for the rest of his life, or possibly going to jail. Somehow no matter what he did, whether he went or not, from the ego's perspective it appeared that he would have to make some kind of sacrifice.

Slowly, over time, Julio saw that his answer was not in his judgment, but rather in his guidance. No matter what his judgment told him, he did not feel peaceful. As he began to quiet himself he was able to listen more to what was within. The focus on consequences lessened and the attention to hearing the answer from within increased.

We often tend to be too concerned with outcomes and not focused enough on our inner process: In the end Julio was not called up for duty. But in any case, he had already made his decision. And what is important is that he quieted his mind, listened to his inner guidance, and accepted what he heard. He took full responsibility for his decision, and felt he was doing the right thing for himself and others.

ASK, LISTEN, TRUST, FOLLOW

Asking is the first task of a four-step process of letting go of judgment and turning our attention inward. It will be followed by *listening, trusting,* and *following.*

In "asking," the first step, we must do so with great intention. We must ask as if we were asking a great teacher the most important question in the world. We must want, more than anything, to hear the answer. At times it may be difficult, but the more we remind ourselves of the following, the more peace of mind we will have:

- I don't know the answer to this question, or what I should do in this situation.
- My personal judgment can be faulty because it is wrapped in the belief in sacrifice.
- If I don't understand the answer I hear I will not discount it. If the answer scares me I will still listen.
- I trust that my guidance will not result in harm to myself or others.
- All that I know, and all that I have learned in the past, may need to be set aside in order for me to follow what I hear. I am willing to do this.

- What other people think does not determine the value of my guidance. I am willing to go "against the crowd" if necessary.
- In following my guidance I must release all resentment and blame.

You might have some resistance to the full impact of what asking will create. It is important to realize that the period of unsettling is born out of not having found consistent peace of mind, even though a sorting out and relinquishment phase has been undertaken. We find that by asking for guidance at this level, we attain the most consistent peace of mind.

Similarly, in "listening," our second step in this process, we must truly listen. Many of us have become accustomed to asking questions while already having in mind the answer that we want to hear. If we don't hear that answer, then either we try to manipulate "our way" into law, or we retreat, feeling rejected or disappointed.

When I was a child a television program called Hogan's Heroes aired weekly. The show featured a character named Sergeant Schultz. Whenever Schultz encountered a situation requiring his judgment he would loudly insist, "I know nothing...I know *nothing*." Though in a slightly different context, it is helpful to say this when attempting to listen to guidance. *It is too often that we can't listen to an answer because what we think about the question gets in the way.*

All of our "shoulds" and "shouldn'ts," concepts of right and wrong, ideas, wants, and desires divert us and get in the way of our listening. Quieting the mind is neccesary if we want to be able to listen.

This book is directed towards quieting the mind so we can listen. Every word and every exercise is geared towards this. The more we practice quieting our mind and listening to our inner guidance, the better we become at it.

In "trusting," the third step in the process of letting go of judgment and turning inward, we come to the crossroads where we must choose to live by the Ego Mind or the Whole Mind. We either listen to judgment or to our inner guidance. The amazing thing is that if we were to rationally look at where our judgment has led us, it would be obvious that we should not invest all of our trust in it. To many, guidance and turning inward are actions that are not grounded in any sort of logic or reason. Yet if you follow your true inner guidance, you will find your life improving. More consistent peace of mind will flourish.

A common trait of a peaceful person is when inner guidance and outer action reflect one another. Following any other tack, we feel dragged or pushed through life, and always have an edge of resentment and anger. Though the content of your guidance might not seem logical or reasonable at the time, the experience that results from following it can easily stand up to reason. For example, does it not seem reasonable and logical to follow and do what leads to more peace in your life, better relationships, and the ability to take more personal responsibility?

The last step in this process consists of "following" what you hear. This is the action step. It is also the step where you will be tempted to strike bargains. You might want to do only part of what you hear in your guidance. You play "Let's Make a Deal." The extent to which you do this is the extent that you do not trust.

Action is very simple if you trust your information. It is quite difficult if you do not. It is important that you don't allow your mind to ask to many "why" or "what-if" questions about your guidance: questions like, "Why would I ever do that?" or, "What if my spouse doesn't agree?" or, "What if I lose something?" The purpose of these questions is usually for the ego to attempt to shoot holes in what you hear from the quiet place inside.

Fear often escalates during this action stage, as it did for Tom, who came to me for psychotherapy several years ago. Tom had always worked for someone else, and he had become accustomed to the security that working for a big company offered. Tom told me that when he first started working at the company that employed him, the work excited him. He looked forward to going to work every day; the issue of financial security was of secondary importance. Yet as time went on, Tom found himself working primarily for the security. The work became less interesting and the challenges also lessened.

In session, when Tom and I would approach the subject of his work, he would usually try to change the subject or in some way move away from his feelings about it. Tom had developed a life outside his work that was very fulfilling. He would often highlight this, hoping that this made his work life seem tolerable.

In truth, most of the people who Tom worked with also felt as he did. Like Tom, they were in managerial positions and would often remind themselves and each other how lucky they were to hold those positions. Although none of them enjoyed work, none of them wanted to consider leaving; even considering the idea of quitting would have seemed foreign to them.

At forty-eight, Tom also believed that he could never "do better" than his present position. He stated that the financial security was very important to him, and he believed that in another job he would never be able to come close to matching his present salary. This belief system prevented him from even the most cursory exploration of his feelings and his own inner guidance. Nothing would be more fearful for him than finding himself without a job. He was sure that everybody in his life would probably have him committed to a mental institution if he ever even spoke of leaving his job.

Slowly in our work together, Tom became less afraid of himself. Eventually, he was able to move through his resistance to looking at his vocational life. One day during an unusual session Tom became overwhelmed and began crying. It was the day that he realized that he had been living out his father's commandment:

"Take care of your family." He was so afraid of doing anything that might let his family down (or his father) that he would not even allow himself to examine any aspect of his work life.

A surprising thing happened for Tom as he opened to exploring all areas of his life. When he would really quiet himself he found that his inner guidance did not prompt him to leave the company. Instead, his guidance led him to work with upper management in ways that would create more challenges and excitement for himself and his colleagues. At first he thought that this new approach seemed crazy, because the structure of the company had been set for so many years. Yet he did not let this fact deter him from suggesting changes, and eventually he presented some of his ideas to his superiors. Today Tom has the same job, but his life is not the same at all. To his great pleasure and surprise, he once again looks forward to going to work each day.

WHAT IS POWER?

Contrary to what many people believe, power is *not* the ability to manipulate and dominate people and our surroundings. Power *is* being aware of who we are and being in touch with our inner life. Personal power lies in seeing the connectedness of all life. And power is often found in yielding rather than dominating. We experience our power when we choose to see the truth rather than to repress it. We are powerful when we choose to heal rather than to attack, because healing comes from love, while attack comes from fear and perceived helplessness. The following outlines the recipes for the two different approaches to personal power:

View of Power: THE EGO MIND

1. Control at all costs.
2. Remember that the end result is more important than the inner process.
3. Analyze every situation.
4. Judge every person.

5. Never admit a mistake.
6. Dominate others.
7. Accumulate as many possessions as possible.
8. Fight, and win, if you think you are being threatened.
9. Figure out the future.
10. Always have a good defense.

View of Power: THE WHOLE MIND ✳

1. Release the past.
2. Be aware of your inner process in each moment.
3. Accept that which you cannot change.
4. Love every person.
5. Embrace your humanness.
6. Accept others.
7. Share as much as possible.
8. Forgive.
9. Be in the moment.
10. Trust in yourself.

Consider the question, *Do I want to see all that I have denied and see the truth of who I am?* You are asking yourself whether the darkness, the shame, and the guilt—which you believe is real and have hidden—truly have any power *in and of themselves.* You are asking yourself whether you want to live in darkness or light. It may also be helpful to look at the question from a slightly different angle. As you look at shame and guilt, ask yourself the following:

Is this what I would see?
Is this the truth of who I am?
Do I want this?

Truly answering these three questions and the one above them cannot happen in one sitting. It's a process. But in answering, you are taking the step necessary to allow yourself to move beyond fear and look within.

You can learn to release your fear, even though it seems as though it controls you. If you choose to see a world where you are no longer helpless, where you have no enemies, the means of releasing your fear will become available to you. In turning within you will find love.

The decision to look within and see the truth of who you are brings a sense of relief and a feeling of calm. Recognition of the truth of who you are adds a dimension of consistency to a life that was previously chaotic. The period of unsettling is, in part, a time of realizing that you had always answered the first three questions with a "yes," but at times would change your mind. Happiness was thus very erratic. By saying "yes" to the fourth question, you are taking the initial steps towards consistent peace of mind.

The period of unsettling can be a very frustrating time if one is unaware that it is simply another stage in the development of trust. It can be frustrating because we begin to realize, despite all of the work, that we haven't really known what was valuable and what was valueless.

Though helpful and necessary, the period of sorting out is not sufficient in developing this knowledge. In the period of relinquishment, we develop the willingness to let go of what is obviously interfering with our peace of mind. At this point however, we don't entirely understand the purpose of the willingness. "In the period of unsettling, which may take some time since its purpose is so contrary to what many of us have learned we are supposed to do, our goal becomes to lay all judgment aside. We can then ask our higher power for guidance in virtually every circumstance that presents itself to us. If the lessons of the each previous periods were not heavily reinforced by greater feelings of peace of mind and a greater ability to trust, this task would be next to impossible." (Please note that the terms higher power, inner guidance, intuition, inner knowing, and God can all be used somewhat interchangeably. I use them all to refer to the voice we can choose to listen to when we choose not to listen to the chatter of the ego.)

YOUR BELIEF IN WHAT YOU ARE

To all those who want to hear the quiet and still voice of love, it will not be drowned out by all of the ego's shouting and senseless arguments. But "the voice you choose to hear . . . depends entirely on your whole belief in what you are."

It's a common belief that love comes and goes in your life and that peace can only be possible a certain percentage of the time. This is not actually so. Love needs no cooperation from you to be itself. Love always exists; yet your *awareness* of it is entirely up to you.

If you choose to listen to and follow what the ego says, you will ultimately see yourself as fragile, in need of constant defense, afraid, and vulnerable. You will see yourself as unsafe in a hostile environment. As a result, you'll experience depression, low self-esteem, a chronic feeling of worthlessness, as well as feelings of intense loneliness. You will believe that you are helpless. Even though you may look very much in control, you will believe that your mind is weak. You will believe that every situation dictates how you should react and that outside forces determine how you feel.

> *"There is another way*
> *of being in the world."*
> Choose to listen
> to another voice.
> *"The Voice of Love"* whispers
> *that you are one with all that is.*

In listening to the guidance of the Whole Mind, you learn that you are safe, and that the power of love can truly heal your mind. You extend compassion rather than building defenses. Your self-esteem is high because you see no value in beating yourself up or holding on to shame. You feel worthwhile because you recognize the value in each and every living thing. There is no feeling of being helpless or out of control, because you recognize that your thinking and your values are totally your own to choose. Your thoughts, not the situation, determine your experience. You recognize that there is nothing in the universe any more powerful than your thinking.

Let us suppose that you find yourself feeling alone or distant from people that you are close to. If you believe that you are as the ego dictates, you will ask questions like: "Where can I find love and what do I have to do to get some?" If you believe you are as the Whole Mind perceives you, you'll ask more appropriate questions like: "What am I placing in front of my awareness of love? What am I afraid of?"

The difference in these questions points to a fundamental difference in belief. In the ego's question, it is assumed that love exists in some places and not in others; that it exists for some, but not for others. There is a belief that one must *do* something in order to *get* love. In contrast, the Whole Mind directs us internally to look at what might be blocking the awareness of love. It is assumed and believed that love exists at all times and is in all places. But our minds can create obstacles that block our ability to experience love.

All of your depression and feelings of being stuck in misery come from one source: the belief that you are separate from others and powerless. In the consultation room, with courageous individuals, I have shared in the exploration of their sense of powerlessness. There is certainly no single way that one adopts feelings of powerlessness. However there are definitely some commonalties in how to rise above them.

Those who find their way out of helplessness ask themselves some very powerful and important questions. In answering these questions they are redefining who they are. Each question also has a large subset of questions, and each of these requires some deep inner searching, to answer. The *full* exploration of these questions can take quite some time, and it can be beneficial to have assistance. Many find in-depth psychotherapy helpful in this regard. Of these life-changing questions, the four primary ones are:

> *Do I desire a life that I rule instead of one where the world rules me?*
> *Do I desire a life in which I am powerful rather than helpless?*
> *Do I desire a life in which I have no enemies?*
> *Do I want to see all that I have denied and see the truth of who I am?*

On the surface the first three questions are probably easy to answer. The last question, if deeply considered, probably brings up a great deal of fear and anxiety. Your reluctance to answer this question shows that you are still afraid of the truth. The ego leads you to believe if you turn inward and trust, you will find a gruesome and dark picture.

You cannot be powerful and at the same time be afraid of who you are. Those who attempt this combination usually become dominant, controlling, dogmatic, and dictatorial. Our history is laced with wars led by such "powerful" individuals. When we try to be powerful while fearing who we are, we always will try to control or conquer our outside world. The fear to look within creates a sense of helplessness, and as a result a sense of impotence underlies one's life.

BEYOND "I WOULD RATHER DO IT MYSELF"

In our culture we harbor the fiercely tenacious belief that independence and self-direction are the highest of all achievements.

For instance, when a wealthy individual is referred to as "self-made," it makes them more "one of us."

Though I believe this problematic idealization of independence holds true across gender lines, in our society it is more firmly established and reinforced in males. Researchers have documented behavior patterns in men that arise out of a societal veneration of self-direction, and some of these behaviors border on the ridiculous. An instance familiar to all of us: A man driving through an unfamiliar city, obviously lost, is nonetheless determined not to ask directions from the locals. Even though he is new to the area, he believes it is better to *find it himself* than to ask for help. For him, somehow, asking for help would be the same as giving up or giving in—a sign of weakness.

The tenet, "Above all else be independent," may be less strictly enforced in the consciousness of women in our society, yet it still presents a problem. Traditionally, women have been kept in confined roles. Because men have more cultural support for being independent, there seems to be no new territory that is off limits to the male (especially the white male). Men are encouraged to "blaze new paths" *on their own*. Women, often, are encouraged to ask for help and assistance. Women are forced to live within primarily male-created roles.

The women's movement has been greatly effective in creating more opportunities for women. Still, it would be tragic if women were to become independent at the cost of giving up their connectedness and ability to ask for assistance. In my practice I have seen many women who either yearn to be released from their confined roles, or who are very successful in what was once a "man's world." Of the women I see in my practice as a psychologist, few have crossed the traditional boundaries without feeling that they somehow lost something in the process. They have lost connectedness—and yearn to find it again.

The fact that both men and women in this culture bend towards independence and away from the need for joining has hardened us and turned our ears away from the gentle voice within. It is time that we, individually and as a culture, begin to recognize our interconnectedness and value our inner guidance.

In our society, we don't think much of answers like, "I meditated on it," or "I asked for inner guidance" as a way of explaining how we made an important decision. We want and expect to hear answers like, "I weighed the alternatives and decided," or "After an analytical and objective critique I came to the logical conclusion." Now, examining objective data and applying reason is certainly a valid way of making many decisions, such as determining the what type of stock to purchase. In our inner lives, however, this method of thinking may rob us of the chance to utilize our *subjective* experience. In other words, logic and reason can deny our emotional and spiritual life.

WHAT WE LEARN AS CHILDREN

What, then, shall we conclude? Shall we teach our children that independence is *not* desirable and that asking for help is the best thing to do in all circumstances? From the above discussion one might think so. But this is not true. Clearly, we have no interest in developing a society full of dependent personalities, and complete suppression of our independence-geared impulses would certainly create such results.

We need to shift our sights to the exploration of how human beings grow and learn. When we look at human beings through a developmental perspective, we can see the need for independence and individuation, and the need for connection and guidance.

We understand, for example, that when the two-year-old toddler pushes away from mommy and says "no" there is a *positive* developmental process occurring. In earlier stages, the infant does not have any sense of separation between self and mother. The young infant has no sense of boundaries, and perceives everything as *connected*. (The Whole Mind also has these qualities, but they are qualitatively more developed. It also contains the added ingredient of self-knowledge.) What the two-year-old is beginning to do is individuate and develop a sense of self; the child is developing independence. As children move through the earlier ages, and even through adolescence, they are continually developing their sense of self. Independent thinking needs to be encouraged. Young children need to do it "their way"—to explore their world on their own terms.

A spiritual life can be initiated early in life, but the child should not be encouraged to ask for inner guidance in all situations, as is being suggested in this period of unsettling. Children need support and encouragement in discovering themselves and exploring their environment. (For the reader who wishes a more complete understanding of theories of development, there are many books addressing this subject in the kind of detail that is beyond the scope of this book. I recommend the writings of educator Jean Piaget and psychologist Eric Ericson as primers.)

Individuation and the gaining of independence are not the end of the developmental process. Many of us—indeed, our whole society—are stuck in our present stage of development. We believe that being in a self-guided and independent state is the highest level of development.

Let's remember that being independent includes the ability to have boundaries and the ability to think on our own. Once we have these abilities we must then, ironically, move beyond them. In the period of unsettling we address the next level of our development. This involves getting our *self,* the "I" aspect of our ego, out of the way so that we may come to listen to our inner guidance and move beyond boundaries and separation.

WILLINGNESS AND THE RESULTS OF LISTENING TO GUIDANCE

By the time you have worked through the first four periods of developing trust, you will very likely feel ready to move on. To do so, you'll need to continue developing a willingness to ask for guidance. The best way to begin is to undertake a full exploration of how your potential has been inhibited because of the compulsion to analyze and judge.

In growing up, I had no real spiritual guidance. My father

was raised in the Jewish faith, my mother as Protestant. Other than an occasional visit to the church or synagogue, God was not talked about. In truth, my parents neither denied God's existence nor encouraged religious belief.

Although I can't know what it would be like to have been raised differently, and although my own children see my wife and me openly pray and meditate, I am actually thankful for my "non-exposure." It has left me more able to approach my spirituality without a lot of excess baggage. Nevertheless, I myself haven't found it easy to ask for guidance on a consistent basis. Interestingly enough, even though every time I do ask for guidance I have a positive experience, it does not immediately lead to my asking for it more frequently. This attests to how easy it is to fall back to the habit of listening to the Ego Mind. And this is why the period of unsettling can take quite a long time to complete. Though I feel that I have made progress, I still struggle with my ego and its resistance to turning to guidance. There is still a part of me that wants to control situations. I want to do it "my way," and be sure that I always have enough information to judge adequately.

The idea of asking for guidance may be new. Let's define just what is meant by asking for guidance, and how it differs from listening to the ego.

Asking for guidance is a *process* rather than an *act* because it encompasses several steps. Eventually this process becomes automatic and incorporated into our daily living so that we do not always have to be forever reminding ourselves to ask for guidance. But this takes time to achieve and, to begin with, we must be vigilant in reminding ourselves. The ego is like a loud and pushy guest at a dinner party making it difficult to listen to anyone else.

The "Ask, Listen, Trust, Follow" process will be useful to you in the search for guidance. It can also help you apply the process in your daily living.

Ask, Listen, Trust, Follow

STEP 1:
"THERE MUST BE A BETTER WAY"

The first step in asking for guidance is wishing to do so in the first place. Certainly, if we believe that the highest level of development is a keen and independent intellect, we will never ask for guidance. We must at least come to a basic willingness to say, "There must be a better and more peaceful way of going through life than always listening to the ego."

The period of unsettling is a type of "hitting bottom" during which we see that the way of the Ego Mind has not served us. At the same time the Ego Mind proclaims that we would be idiots to abandon it. In the eyes of the ego, turning to guidance is equivalent to stepping off a cliff overlooking a bottomless pit.

At this stage of the period of unsettling, inner conflict is great. We ask ourselves, "How can I have done so much work and still be unhappy?" Despair increases, and for a while hope decreases. Then we finally come to a place of true willingness to see that there is another way.

Typically, this turbulent stage is not limited to a onetime occurrence. The ego tends to rear its dying head a number of times during our lifetime. I consider several different times during my own life to be periods of unsettling. One of these became an important turning point for me.

Years ago, when my former wife and I separated, I thought that the world had come crashing to an end. I was in great despair and all of my "self-development" seemed to have flown out the window. I experienced only the depths of depression, hopelessness, and sadness. I felt as if I had no direction. I was unemployed, and had no money and no place to live. I felt that no one was able to understand what I was experiencing. And every passing day magnified my feelings of loneliness. I was even tempted to return to drug use, but fortunately there was some part of me that knew I would rise above all that which was taking place.

Long before the separation I had begun a daily practice

of meditation. I had been involved in therapy, and had my doctorate in psychology. None of this seemed to be helpful to me at this point. One day as I drove down the side of Mount Tamalpias from my therapist's office, I had a sudden experience that God was with me and that through God's guidance there was a different way of being in the world. Certainly, all of my emotional pain did not suddenly disappear. Yet there was a sense of companionship and purpose that had not previously existed. Before that life-changing moment I did not want anything to do with God; because of dishonest actions on my part that had lead to my marriage splitting up, I felt very guilty and completely undeserving.

STEP 2:
TURNING AWAY FROM THE EGO

As we've discused, when we recognize that there must be a better way to live our ego will still loudly proclaim that we are crazy to turn away from its guidance. To move on in our development we need to adopt a willingness to quiet our mind from the chatter of the ego. We must be willing to do this despite constant setbacks. The ego's voice often dominates, and it can take you some time to be able to consistently quiet your mind.

Self-mastery can be defined simply as the ability to quiet the mind and listen with complete awareness. Like any kind of mastery, it takes dedication and persistence. The following techniques represent ways that you can begin to practice quieting your mind. Try them all and then choose one or two that work best for you. Continue with those awhile before switching to other techniques. At first glance, some of these methods may seem awkward or silly. At these times, remember that you have had a great deal of education in analytical thought, but probably not much on how to quiet your automatic thinking and the ego's chatter. Though the act of quieting the mind may be foreign, it's a necessary step in the development of your ability to listen to your inner guidance.

CONSCIOUS BREATHING

As mentioned earlier, the use of the breath is a powerful tool in quieting the mind. Sit comfortably with your back erect yet relaxed. Place your feet flat on the floor and have your hands loosely by your side or folded in your lap. With your eyes closed begin by simply observing your breath. Do not try and change your breathing in any way, simply watch it. After a few minutes check to see if your breath is full and extending into your abdomen. If not, deepen your breathing. Each cycle of breath should be slow, smooth, and uninterrupted. As you watch your breath you may notice that it is difficult to control your mind racing from thought to thought. Simply bring your focus of attention back to your breathing whenever you find yourself stuck on an unwanted thought. Imagine that upon your exhalation you can release all of your thoughts.

Focus upon one aspect of your breath. For example, place your attention on the point between when you inhale and exhale; the point where you are not quite inhaling, but not exhaling yet either. Do not stop your breathing, just focus your attention at this point. Or, as an alternative, you can focus your attention on the soft and barely audible sound that your breathing makes. One other point of focus might be the area between your upper lip and nose, where the sensation of the air entering and exiting your nostrils can be felt.

Remember, the key here is practice. The more you do this, the more you will find a peaceful feeling resulting from it. Try not to give in to initial frustration.

THE USE OF A STATEMENT

Focus on one statement in a repetitive fashion in order to let all other thoughts slip away. This technique has also been referred to as using *affirmations,* and is related to the use of *mantras.* The principle is the same in each: By repetitive and attentive focus on one particular word or idea, we enable ourselves to move *inward* with it.

Though the specific word or phrase you choose can vary, it is important that it does not carry negative messages with it. To begin with, I suggest that you use one of the lesson titles from this book. Another suggestion that many have found helpful is to simply use the word *one* as the focus of attention.

With your eyes closed and your breathing relaxed and deep, begin to silently repeat to yourself the phrase or word that you have chosen. You can attach the word or phrase to each inhalation and exhalation. For example, if using the word "one," say "one," as you inhale, and then again as you exhale. As with all the exercises in this book, if you find yourself sidetracked, thinking about something else, gently bring your attention back to what you are intending to do. Though you may start out with five-minute practice periods, it is helpful on all of the techniques to work up to about twenty minutes.

WALKING MEDITATION

Many people find it difficult to sit for extended periods of time without a lot of chatter in their minds. In a walking meditation, the focus centers on each movement of each step. Walk very slowly, preferably alone, and say to yourself exactly what each movement is. As you lift your foot from the ground say, "lifting foot." As you move it forward say, "stepping forward." As your foot touches the ground say, "foot touching ground," and so on. This technique allows you to move yet is very quieting and centering as well.

THOUGHT NAMING

This approach is particularly helpful for those who say, "No matter what I do, I just can't control my thoughts." With this technique, instead of fighting and controlling your thoughts, you simply watch and name them as they come and go. In doing so, it is important that you have a mental stance that is as detached as possible. Simply watch your thoughts and state what the thought is about. Think of it as if you were watching a movie, with the task of naming each scene and then going on to the next. Let's imagine, for example, that you are sitting with your eyes closed and you begin to think about work. Say to yourself, "Thinking about work," and then go on to whatever else pops into your mind. Try not to delve into any one thought. Just name it and go on to the next. The practice of nonattachment to each thought will allow you to become mentally still.

The previous three approaches—breath, a phrase, or movement—are used to focus our attention. This thought-naming exercise is based on the same principle, but here we use thoughts themselves to focus our attention.

EXTERNAL FOCUS OF ATTENTION

We have all had the experience of staring into a fire and becoming mesmerized with the flickering flames. In this approach we use an external object to focus our attention. Once our thoughts are quiet, we can continue to turn within. Though any object will do, even a spot on the wall or a star in the sky, the single flame of the candle is an easy object to practice with because it is so captivating.

When looking at the flame allow yourself to focus all of your attention upon it, as if it is the only thing in all of the world. Don't take your eyes off of it. You may find it helpful to repeat the phrase "my mind is still" as you concentrate on the flame.

PHYSICAL FOCUSING

Here the body is used as the object of our attention. Through a combination of the walking meditation and thought-naming exercises, you focus upon any body sensation that you may have, while avoiding becoming attached to it. This is also a very good technique to accomplish because it is an excellent tool for controlling pain.

To begin, let's imagine that you have a slight itch or mild discomfort in your left leg. Focus your attention on that sensation and state to yourself, "hurting, hurting, hurting" or "itching, itching, itching," until it either ceases or changes. Any physical discomfort can become a focal point of our awareness and can help you to quiet your mind.

It is only when we become future oriented that the discomfort begins to control us. If we begin to think, "When is this pain going to stop?" or "I can't take this any more," then we become captive to the discomfort. When we acknowledge the discomfort in the present moment without extending the pain into the future, it ceases to have power over us. If you have ever had sudden onset of pain, such as hitting your finger with a hammer, you know that your mind is not thinking about a lot of things in that moment other than the pain. In this approach we use a lesser degree of discomfort to our advantage and use body sensations as a means of focusing our attention and quieting our minds.

STEP 3:
ASKING FOR GUIDANCE,
NOT EXTERNAL RESULTS,
WITHOUT ATTACHMENT

It's important to understand what guidance is, and what it is not. In the previous discussion on *asking,* a series of questions were presented to assist you in being able to ask for guidance in a genuine and deep way. Here I would like to expand on this idea by introducing two other aspects.

Many of us are very "results" oriented. We look for tangible and external indicators of progress. In asking for guidance we must let go of this narrow way of judging progress. The Whole Mind does not view time in the same way that the Ego Mind does. In asking for guidance, therefore, we may hear direction that has no apparent immediate value. Here we must adopt the faith that listening to our guidance will result in a positive outcome. Remember the goal of listening to guidance is always peace of mind.

Our ego furthermore tends to ask questions with the answer it wants to hear already in mind. Non-attachment is a prerequisite to asking for guidance. Otherwise we will influence the results of what we hear. In scientific research there is a phenomenon known as experimenter bias, in which the experimenter's beliefs influence what he or she will find. Even in the most controlled situations, the preconceived ideas of what the results will be can influence the outcome. In the same way, in asking for guidance, we must identify and attempt to set aside any preconceived ideas.

About a year ago I had some disagreements with a good friend. We both thought we were right about a situation involving the return of money for a loan. At the time I wanted what I thought was right, but I also valued the friendship. As time went on the tension within me and between us seemed to worsen; my friend and I were growing distant. My inner guidance led me to focus on the compassion that I felt for this person, and not let other matters get in the way. But this did not mean simply giving up my position. It meant believing that I didn't have to get angry and defensive just because somebody disagreed with me. Even though the other person chose to distance himself by not communicating, I still experienced love for him.

Recently I received a letter from my friend. He wrote that, over the year, he had often thought about the conflict between us. In reading the letter, my Ego Mind experienced a sense of satisfaction that our disagreement had made my friend uncomfortable, and that I was being seen as right by people around me. As I quieted my mind, I realized that the only important thing was my acknowledging his willingness to reach out and to work on forgiveness.

To my ego this made no sense. If I had listened to my ego, my concern would have been being right. But by setting this kind of thinking aside, I was able to listen to my inner guidance regarding how to proceed in a loving yet assertive manner. If I had been "results oriented," I would have thought that whatever course led to my getting what I wanted was the best one.

Through this and many other experiences I have come to learn that attending to my inner life and my inner guidance is of the utmost importance. It is the source of my growth. I am the only one who can journey within myself; no one else can experience my inner life in place of me. It is my fundamental responsibility to ask for guidance without attachment. To stay with my guidance, and to move from the ego, requires me to have faith in something that is not familiar or necessarily tangible. I must believe that my inner process and guidance will lead me to something richer and more fulfilling than what the ego has. The more I turn inward, the greater the possibility of consistent peace of mind.

The most significant discoveries that I have made in my life have come from turning within. Listening to love rather than listening to fear has brought peace in times of conflict. When I have supported myself in this process I have always found purpose and meaning where only confusion and fear existed previously.

STEP 4:
LISTENING TO AND TRUSTING THE ANSWER

The following are guidelines to follow to ensure that you are able to listen to guidance after turning inward and asking. They are meant to help you trust what you hear from your inner guidance.

GUIDELINES FOR TRUSTING AND FOLLOWING YOUR INNER GUIDANCE

1. Refrain from judging by what you see on the surface.
2. Do not ask a question and then plug your ears because you're afraid of the answer.
3. Remember that you do not have to understand something in order for it to have truth.
4. Don't listen and judge. Listen and trust.
5. You can only hear love when you let go of fear.

6. You cannot listen to loving guidance while condemning yourself.
7. You cannot blame others and listen to guidance within.
8. See possibilities for healing instead of obstacles to love.
9. Set aside other people's voices so you can hear your own.
10. Listen with the heart.
11. Trust in what creates joining, not in what creates separation.
12. Remember that you cannot really listen as long as you hold onto expectations or specific outcomes to situations.
13. Keep in mind that you cannot be impatient and be able to really listen.
14. It is most difficult to trust while holding onto the past.
15. Only when you're willing to let go of old beliefs can you listen.
16. To be able to listen and trust you cannot have attachment to being right.
17. Assumptions about yourself and others cloud your ability to hear.
18. If you believe that you are alone, in a world of scarcity, you will generally look for information to support this belief.
19. It is hard to listen and trust if you focus on what you are going to "get."
20. It is impossible to listen and trust when you have a closed mind. You must believe that anything is possible and that there are no limitations on yourself or others.
21. Guidance always includes forgiveness. If you place value in attack and defense you will not be able to trust your guidance.

22. If you see yourself as weak you will think
    that your guidance is asking more of you
    than you can give, and you will not trust it.

"THE PERIOD OF ACHIEVEMENT"

This period is an unusual one: it is not marked by any task or by our having to do anything more. It is more a state of mind, a final mental outlook, an unwavering attitude in which we rest. The period of achievement should not be seen as static or an end, for it holds the potential for endless depth and growth.

For so long my mind was a tornado of confusion.
Now all fragmentation begins to end.
For so long it seemed that there were so many
    different lessons to learn,
now all learning is consolidated.
My faith was once like reluctant shadows in a
    shaded corner,
difficult to count on, fearful, and easy to
    overlook.
Now my little steps have become giant strides
    and solid gains.
Turning inward is natural, fear is distant.
Hiding who I am is but an old habit that has
    been outgrown,
I would not want to hide even if I could.
Consistency of thought more readily travels
    with me,
where once my mind moved in dark isolation
    from one illusion to another.
The way now is not without obstacles,
yet the path is clear for me to follow and I trust
    my steps.
Tranquility has tamed my anger.
When tranquility arrives,
who would seek to exchange it for something else?
What can be more desirable than this?

PART

II

Traits That Rest on Trust

After having gone through the steps of developing trust, we may begin building upon trust as a foundation. We now turn our attention to the traits—the aspects of ourselves that set the direction or "mood" of the way we live—that rest on trust.

As trust is established, we can then develop the traits in ourselves that lead to a deeper and more loving life. These traits include honesty, tolerance, gentleness, joyousness, defenselessness, generosity, patience, and open-mindedness. Until trust begins to be established, these traits can only be experienced in an artificial way. Trust allows us to truly explore who we are—the depths of ourselves—and to develop our potential.

Following a discussion of each trait you will find daily lessons. These daily lessons are designed to help you to practice and more firmly establish each of these traits in your daily being. It is recommended that you proceed with the lessons as outlined on page 72.

Honesty

*Although we are reluctant to believe that
our own actions and attitudes have been the cause of
our pain, eventually we cannot ignore this conflict.*
Tarthang Tulka in
Gesture of Balance

Most of us tend to think of honesty in terms of words, and that if we "tell the truth," we are being honest. But this definition of honesty needs to be broadened, for *real honesty means consistency between what we say, what we do, and what we think. A Course in Miracles* eloquently expands this idea:

> *There is nothing you say that contradicts what you*
>   *think or do;*
> *no thought opposes any other thought;*
> *no act belies your word;*
> *and no word lacks agreement with another.*
> *Such are the truly honest.*
> *At no level are they in conflict with themselves.*
> *Therefore it is impossible for them to be in conflict*
>   *with anyone or anything.*

In an earlier book of mine, *Healing the Addictive Mind,* I discussed my use of drugs and how my life was affected by it. I remember the day, during that period of my life, that I finally decided to tell other people in my life about what I had been doing—the drugs, the secrecy, the dishonesty—and about my isolation. I had been seeing a psychologist for a number of months. We both decided that it would be beneficial for me to meet with the two people whom I was most afraid to tell about my drug use: my father and my physician.

My doctor had been a man with whom I had been very close. From the time I was fifteen until I turned twenty-one, he had been an emotional anchor in my life. I knew that he deeply cared for me not only as a patient, but also as an individual. The problem was that I had been lying to him for years in order to get drugs and emotional support and sensitivity. I had faked pain, purposely got in car accidents, and used many other methods to continue to get drugs. At the same time, I felt tremendous guilt over this behavior: What I really wanted was love, but I did not know how to stop the vicious cycle I'd become involved in.

To compound the problem, when I met with my father and my doctor, I was also harboring the mistaken belief that all I needed to do was to "come clean," to tell them what had been happening. Then I would magically become an honest person. I believed my confession was all that would be required of me to become honest.

To my surprise, however, meeting with them and telling them the truth was merely the first step in a journey of many years that led to trust and honesty. I would learn that having the intention of being honest is positive, but it is the practice itself—consistently being responsible to ourselves, other people, and the planet—that truly leads to honesty.

At the time of my confession, I remember being angry at my father and my doctor for not immediately congratulating me on the new direction I was taking with my life. Though supportive, they were, at the same time, upset and distrusting of me; I had been lying to them off and on for years. My doctor was quite angry at me, and he discontinued much of our professional and personal relationship. At the time this was very painful for me because I don't think he really knew how important his friendship was to me. I felt that being honest resulted in my losing my anchor to sanity.

With continued self-exploration I found that what I really needed to do was to stop condemning myself and forgive myself. As my wish to deceive myself and others about who I was and what I was doing decreased, I found that I was able to be gentler and more forgiving with myself. Forgiveness, in turn, allowed honesty to be born, for it is impossible to be honest and unforgiving at the same time: To be *unforgiving* we must be condemning, and to condemn ourselves or others is dishonest. The most honest thing we can do is to see ourselves not from the viewpoint of the judging past or the fearful future, but in the light of the present moment.

LESSON THREE

"Forgiveness ends the dream of conflict here."

In order to have honesty in our daily lives we must address the notion of conflict, which I define broadly as any state of mind other than peace of mind. The conflicted mind cannot be truly honest: Peace of mind is our natural state; an absence of it indicates a form of internalized conflict. The following questions will help you explore how you have dealt with conflict in the past:

1. Have you at any time in your life experienced conflict between another person and yourself but were afraid to address it?
2. Do you ever do things you don't believe in to avoid conflict?
3. Have you ever internalized a conflict instead of addressing it, or blamed another person for it?
4. Do you ever "gloss over" a conflict in order to "keep the peace?"
5. Are you ever deceitful or manipulative with yourself or others in order to avoid conflict?

If we want honesty, conflict cannot be disguised, denied, evaded, hidden, or seen somewhere else. Honesty implies resolving conflict, accepting our true and natural state, which is peace of mind. To resolve conflict in our life we must be willing to recognize conflict of any kind when it presents itself. We must be willing to examine those thoughts of ours that created the conflict. Only when we do this are we able to lift all of the defenses that we have had, for defensiveness does not allow for honesty.

Today's lesson asks you to commit to changing the way you have dealt with conflict. It is devoted to identifying the conflicts in your life today. They may be old beliefs and feelings from childhood, or they could be a situation taking place right now.

Begin making a list of things that you feel unforgiving about, conflicts that involve both yourself and others. Spend a fair amount of time with this. You may want to leave it and come back to it throughout the day.

Your first task will be to recognize issues that are unresolved in your life. An example of a list might be:

1. I am angry about my sister leaving home early.
2. I don't like my job, but I stay there because it is secure.
3. There is tension between my spouse and me, though I pretend that everything is all right.

When you have completed your list ask yourself if you are truthfully willing to deal with these issues differently than you have in the past. Doing so will mean committing yourself to *resolving* conflict rather than *avoiding* it.

Begin by closing your eyes. Then, one by one, picture the person or people involved in each of the predicaments that you wrote down. Don't forget to include yourself. Say to yourself:

> *"Forgiveness is the light you choose to shine away all conflict and all doubt, ... No light but this can ..."* end the conflict that I have been carrying.

Remember that if you hold on to blame, the conflict cannot be resolved. Commit yourself today to directly resolving any conflict, new or old, that arises with another person. With forgiveness as your base, you no longer have to be afraid to address the issues that so deeply affect your daily living.

LESSON FOUR

"Love holds no grievances."

In the preceding lesson we learned that forgiveness leads to peace. Today we look at the other side of the equation: the fact that holding grievances *always* leads to guilt.

To know oneself is to be honest. We cannot truly know ourselves as long as we hold grievances; they are like iron doors hiding the light of forgiveness from our minds.

Holding grievances means forgetting that we are love itself. When we are holding on to grievances we are letting the Ego Mind rule our lives. Because the Ego Mind uses denial, blame, and projection as its primary tools, it is clearly dishonest. Today it is important to see the effects that holding grievances has upon our minds. When we clearly see this we will be sufficiently motivated to let them go.

Holding grievances means that we are denying that we are worthy of love. We cannot condemn and at the same time feel any sense of unity. When we hold on to grievances, we are seeing ourselves as split off from our higher power, and other people. In short, holding grievances shuts us off from knowing ourselves. Giving even one grievance any power begins a whole series of attack thoughts—of blaming—all of which lead to fear and separation. Holding on to grievances is nothing short of denying love.

When we hold grievances we forget who we are.
When we forgive we will remember.

You may be reading this thinking that you cannot possibly release all your grievances. Yet relinquishing is simply a matter of motivation and belief.

Today your goal is to find out how you would feel without your grievances. If you succeed in doing so, even ever so slightly, you will never have a motivation problem again. You will never have to wonder if you want to be honest; it will cease to even be a question.

As with the previous lessons, begin today with searching your mind for people you hold major grievances towards. Next, look for minor grievances that you hold towards those you like, and even love. You will quickly see that there are few people towards whom you do not hold some grievance. This is what makes you feel alone.

Today, determine to see all of these people as your friends, whether you know them well or not. One by one, say to them:

> *I choose to see you as my friend,*
> *so that I may remember that you are not*
> *separate from me.*
> *By doing so I come to know myself.*

With your eyes closed, spend about ten minutes envisioning yourself totally at peace with everyone and everything. You are perfectly safe in a world that loves you, and that you love. Feel the safety that surrounds you. Believe that nothing can harm your peace of mind. After the ten minutes say to yourself:

> *"Love holds no grievances.*
> *When I let all my grievances go*
> *I will know I am perfectly safe."*

Practice the lesson in quick application whenever any grievance arises against anyone. It does not matter whether they are physically present. Say to yourself:

> *"Love holds no grievances.*
> *Let me not betray my Self."*

Tolerance

*And let there be no purpose in friendship save
the deepening of the spirit.*
Kahlil Gibran in
The Prophet

Tolerance implies a refrainment from judgment, and is the direct result of the application of the principles that have been presented thus far. Specifically:

*"To judge is to be dishonest, for to judge is to
assume a position you do not have."*

We are all equal in our desire for love, our worthiness in receiving love, and our underlying ability to forgive. "To judge is to be dishonest" because it denies this truth; in lieu of it, we hold ourselves to be superior (if we are judging others), or inferior (if we are judging ourselves). Since, in truth, we are neither superior nor inferior to our fellow human beings, to judge assumes a position we do not have.

"God's teachers do not judge."

In looking at tolerance I have found it helpful to have role models. Without these role models, tolerance can remain a distant concept. In my life, two such role models have been the Dalai Lama and Mother Teresa. Each of them demonstrate to me that it is possible to walk through life with a minimum of judgment. As a result they radiate peace. I remind myself that these two people are no different from anyone else. They are simply human beings who have chosen to adopt a perception of the world that is love-based rather than fear-based. There is no reason that each of us cannot begin to do the same.

In my work as a psychologist, I often see people who keep long inventories of the ways in which their spouses are intolerant and critical. As with all of the traits that rest on trust, the best way to receive tolerance from others is to develop tolerance in ourselves. It is like a magical solution: When we refrain from being judgmental the world immediately becomes a much safer place for us. Just as tolerance breeds tolerance, judgment breeds judgment. If I say, "I will love you as soon as you are more tolerant of me," I am keeping myself stuck in the Ego Mind. It is through extending love, not waiting for it, that tolerance becomes present in our lives.

"Judgment without self-deception is impossible."

We often believe that holding judgmental thoughts toward ourselves and others means being fiercely honest about who we are, and making sure not to deceive ourselves—yet nothing could be further from the truth.

The Whole Mind reflects the truth about who we are, and that is love. The Ego Mind is based on fear, which is illusion. This means that when you judge you are deceiving yourself. When we view ourselves and others through the eyes of love we do not need to "try" to be tolerant. It will come naturally. Likewise, in judgment love escapes our awareness and fear fills our mind.

"Judgment implies a lack of trust," and 'trust is the foundation of the Whole Mind.'

Without trust love cannot express itself: We become trapped in a fearful dream that the ego convinces us is real. If you want to learn the lessons of love you must be willing to relinquish judgment. Judgment virtually destroys honesty and does away with trust.

So many people want intimacy, yet because of judgment are afraid of it. In our marriage, my wife Carny and I are currently focusing in on our tolerance with one another. We were recently blessed with a new child, and we moved to a larger home. Both of these are wonderful things in our life, yet both certainly produce stress. We found ourselves becoming increasingly short with one another, and, largely unconsciously, were judging and blaming each other. The degree of our low tolerance would seem inconsequential to many; however, we have found that lack of tolerance tends to snowball rather quickly. There is no judgmental thought, no matter how small it may seem, that does not block the flow of love. Realizing that we wanted love to be the guide in our relationship we decided to make a commitment to catching ourselves when we became short and intolerant. It is amazing how simply having the commitment to move in the direction of love allows our whole relationship to shift in focus. It is enlivening to feel love flow into our hearts when a day before we might have been intolerant. I suggest that such a shift in focus is possible in all of our relationships, all of the time. It is a matter of choice and discipline.

I might add that a commitment to tolerance does not mean that things that bother us are not discussed. It means that uncomfortable issues are discussed with the desire to love one another rather than judge each other.

LESSON FIVE

"In fearlessness and love I spend today."

This pledge is a commitment to tolerance. Letting go of fear allows love to shine in our lives. With love, we are tolerant. With fear, we are defensive and judgmental. Decide today that there is simply no room in your life for judgment. This is the only thing that you need to concentrate upon today. It is more important than anything else.

In today's lesson you seek to know the difference between imprisonment and freedom. When you have judged, you may have thought that you were defending your freedom, your independence. Yet all that you were doing was tightening the shackles around your heart.

The Ego Mind does not know what it is trying to teach you. Its only expertise is in confusion. When you listen to the chatter of the ego telling you to judge, it is as though you are listening to the wind but thinking that you are hearing voices. The ego is nothing. It is based upon fear alone, and only false perception can follow.

You have free will. You can choose to be free in fearlessness and love, or imprisoned in fear and judgment. Today exercise your power of decision. Begin by closing your eyes and thinking of all of the things that you are afraid of, and all of the judgments that you may hold. You may be fearful about finances, or be judging yourself or someone for something in the past. Spend about five minutes, and be as specific as you can. Then say to yourself:

"All of these fears and judgments have
nothing to do with who I am, or who others are.
Today I seek tolerance.
'In fearlessness and love I spend today.'"

Doing so does not mean that you don't address the things you are fearful about. Rather, it is by letting go of these fears that you can really reclaim your personal power. Without fear we are free to address concerns in our lives. Letting go of preoccupation with the future greatly reduces fear. Free of fear, we recognize what is within our ability to change and what is not. Free of fear, acceptance of ourselves and others comes streaming into our lives, as sunlight would enter a dark room. Through acceptance we find tolerance.

As I've said, letting go of judgment doesn't mean that you do not address conflicts with others. You simply approach them *without blaming*. Whenever feelings arise of judgment, blame, or intolerance towards yourself or others, say:

> *"I will not imprison myself today. I choose freedom*
> *by extending love and forgiveness."*

LESSON SIX

"Only my condemnation injures me."

Today we continue with yesterday's discussion of what brings us freedom or imprisonment. Begin by repeating the sentence below several times. Then, with your eyes closed, contemplate its application to your life:

> *"Condemn and you are made a prisoner.*
> *Forgive and you are freed."*

If we fully believed this and practiced this, we would never be without peace of mind.

Why would we want to injure anyone? Why would we limit our potential in any way? Today we begin our healing. We do this through letting go of all condemning and limiting thoughts. As we know, wounds that are not cleaned will not heal. In the same way, our minds cannot be healed until we clean them of all condemnation. And as always, forgiveness provides the means by which we cleanse our minds.

Forgiveness is the gentle "letting go" that allows all dreams of disaster and judgment to disappear. If you are suffering in any way, you are undoubtedly harboring an unforgiving thought that needs to be brought before the light of the Whole Mind.

Only one thing stands between you and the peace of mind that comes with tolerance: your attachment to your belief that judgment offers you something that you want. Even while you hold on to such an irrational thought, the stillness of your true self remains unharmed. Even while you continue to hurt yourself, your true self is fully forgiving, waiting for you to turn your gaze away from the ego and open your heart.

Help pave the way to your own freedom today. Any time you are aware of any feeling other than perfect tranquility and tolerance, say to yourself:

"Only my condemnation injures me.
Only my own forgiveness sets me free."

Now is the time to declare your freedom. Decide today to wait no longer.

Gentleness

*When you express gentleness and precision
in your environment, then real brilliance and power can
descend onto that situation.*
Chogyam Trungpa in
Shambala

Gentleness is like a calm morning breeze that softly awakens us to the new day. Gentleness never employs force; it gets its power instead from yielding. It is not necessarily passive: its strength is derived from persistence. Gentleness nourishes us like a light spring rain, washing away our judgmental thoughts and leaving only radiance.

The ego uses the weapons of guilt and shame to convince us that gentleness is a weakness instead of a sign of strength. The mind that holds on to guilt cannot be trusting; peace of mind becomes impossible. How can we adopt a genuine attitude of gentleness toward ourselves while believing that we are guilty or shameful? Judgment, shame, and guilt create a mind that has bars locking gentleness and serenity out. To the mind that is guilty, the fear of attack lurks everywhere. And when we are expecting attack at any moment, gentleness is a luxury we cannot afford. I've diagramed the specific differences between the Ego Mind and the Whole Mind below:

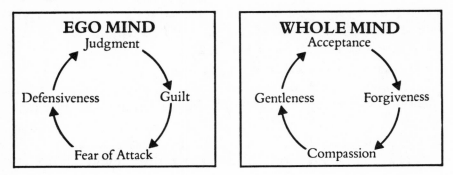

Not long ago a client came to see me. Laura had been in a series of unsuccessful relationships with men. Though she was a very attractive woman in her late thirties, during our first visits her thick dark hair half-covered her face, as though she were peeking around a curtain, trying to see if it was safe to come out. She seemed to use her smile to keep a safe distance between herself and me, and never really addressed her authentic feelings. I remember that by the time she left the first session, there was not one bit of genuine feeling in the room—yet her deep hidden sadness lingered in the air.

I worked with Laura over a period of two years. By allowing herself to begin being gentle with herself, she transformed her guarded distance into a genuineness.

During Laura's years growing up, her father was a very talented and respected architect. Within the small community in which they lived, he was looked upon as a very intelligent person, a hard-working community member, and a true "family man." In actuality, at home he was critical, self-absorbed, and verbally abusive. Laura had a most difficult time revealing that her father had made many sexual gestures towards her throughout her adolescence. Because he had not physically handled her, she assumed that there was no abuse and felt that she could not tell anyone about it. By repeatedly clarifying that he never touched her, she minimized the importance of his behavior and of her own feelings about it.

In the family home, Laura learned to be very guarded. She never knew when some disaster would occur. She believed that in order to protect herself she needed to be constantly vigilant about his mood. Her parents had always taught her, "Never say no to your parents." For Laura, a paradox developed: how do you *not* do what you know is wrong when you can't say no?

Midway through our work together, Laura began mentioning frequently how much she had progressed. Her evidence of the improvement was that she had become very good at protecting herself. This self-protection did indeed represent progress: Laura was more able to refrain from involving herself in relationships with people—especially men—who were not right for her. Previously if someone wanted to date her or spend time with her, she felt an obligation to say yes.

At the same time, however, she still held the belief that she was constantly in *need* of protection. She became very guarded and always feared some form of demands by other people. With fear and guardedness as the primary ways she operated in the world, gentleness towards herself and others was still quite absent.

The ability to be on guard and protect herself had allowed Laura to survive her childhood. As an adult these "survival tools" kept her from happiness. In order to adopt an attitude of gentleness, she had to begin to see that she was not, in fact, in need of constant protection. This step scared her. She had always believed that good protection was what would make the world a safe place. The idea that gentleness could create safety was new for her.

To further her progress she had to learn the difference between assertiveness and protection. The Ego Mind tells us that we should fear the future. It proclaims that every negative thing that has happened to us will most likely occur again if we do not defend ourselves and have limitless protection. In contrast, the Whole Mind asserts that gentleness is a result of following our inner guidance *in the moment*. This is in stark contrast to being in the protection mode. More specifically, the difference in messages sent by the Whole Mind and the Ego Mind in this regard are as follows:

THE EGO MIND

- Look to the past and then project this fearful past onto the future.
- Guard yourself *at all times*; otherwise you will get hurt.
- Defend and you are safe.

THE WHOLE MIND

- In the present moment quiet your mind.
  Turn inward and ask yourself, "What is right
  for me *right now*?"
- Listen to your inner guidance. Be gentle and
  forgiving with yourself and others.
- Gentleness creates safety.

You may feel that these guidelines suggest that people should dissolve their boundaries, or that it is all right to let others walk all over us. Yet this is not the message.

Let's return to the previous case. By consistently turning inward for guidance rather than to the past, Laura became more able to trust herself and know what was right for her. In turn, she began to trust her ability to assert herself. This allowed her to let go of her attitude of being on guard and in constant need of protection. She was able to trust that she could handle any situation, in the moment, should it arise.

Herein lies an important and fundamental difference between assertiveness and protection: *Assertiveness is based on the present moment and feeling confident that one can voice what is right for them, and if needed, protect themselves from harm. The attitude of protection is one of a constant fear that limits our ability to react in the moment.*

As described earlier on page 59, in the martial art of Seibukan Jujutsu there is a practice called *henka. Henka* is based on *kan*, a word which roughly translates as "intuition." In the practice of *henka* one takes all that one knows about the totality of one's being and applies it to conflict situations without having *thinking* in the way. One learns to trust and implement skills without need of being constantly on guard. In *henka*, the true martial artist is relaxed, supple, and without fear, regardless of what is coming his or her way. This allows the practitioner to react to the situation *as it is,* rather than from fear of *what it might be.*

Though Laura was not a student of the martial arts, in essence she became very good at the *attitude* of *henka*. She was able to begin to walk through her life with gentleness. At the same time she trusted that she could now assert herself and not be emotionally violated in any way.

CAUSING HARM

Intentionally causing harm to another being always has an effect upon us. Harmful behavior or thinking completely wipes out trust. In its place confusion, fear, anger, and suspicion prosper. *No gain can come from being harmful: not to ourselves, others, or the planet.* Once we accept this fact, we are then ready to delve deeper into its profound meaning.

In order to truly adopt gentleness we must let go of any value that we see in guilt. When we believe in guilt we are being harmful. Anytime we are being negatively judgmental towards ourselves or others, we are being harmful. In essence, being harmful is the dishonest act that follows a dishonest judgmental thought.

When we come from gentleness we are doing something very important. We are believing that there is no situation, no relationship, and no event that does not occur for the purpose of learning.

Through criticism and judgment we deny ourselves the opportunity to learn. Yet our quest is to learn and grow, to glean all that gentleness has to offer. The following quote from *A Course in Miracles* gives a beautiful summation of the power and impact of gentleness. Each day, before beginning the daily lessons in this section, read this quietly to yourself:

> ... *realize that harm can actually achieve nothing.*
> *No gain can come of it.*
> ... *who would choose the weakness*
> *that must come from harm in place of the unfailing,*
> *all-encompassing and limitless strength of*
> > *gentleness?*

LESSON SEVEN

"Let me be still and listen to the truth."

Gentleness comes from a quiet place within you. Today, lay aside the ego's voice. In exchange receive the gift of gentleness, which is strong in stillness and certain in its direction.

Take some time and experience your life as it is this moment. Recognize all of the pain and confusion that has traveled with you when you have directed your attention to the ego. No matter how loudly it shouts, the voice of the ego is not a trusting guide. It won't lead you to peace of mind. When you have valued the valueless you have been chasing illusions. How can you ever find the peace that you are looking for in such a pursuit?

Commit yourself to taking three fifteen-minute practice periods today. During each practice, sit comfortably with your eyes closed. Deepen your breathing and begin to relax. Let go of any unwanted thoughts. Bring the focus of your attention back to the smooth and rhythmic sound of your breath.

"Be still today and listen to the truth." Choose to listen to your inner guidance. You may not hear actual words, you may simply feel more of a sense of peace and relaxation. Know that your inner teacher is there patiently waiting for you to listen. Know that you have deceived yourself in your previous pursuits for happiness in the valueless. Today turn away from the Ego Mind.

Begin to listen to a new voice, offering a new direction founded in gentleness. Let go of all the voices of the world instructing you to "buy this" or "crave that," claiming that you are somehow deficient. Walk quietly past fear. Extend a welcome hand to love. Commit yourself to becoming a messenger of gentleness, rather than a judge. Don't condemn yourself and others with the life sentence of guilt. A gentle glance to another, a soft smile where you may have once condemned, all of this rewards you a thousandfold today.

Turn inward and ask what you may give today. Become a joyous giver rather than a fearful seeker, and you will find peace of mind. Practice giving in a new way. In each practice period begin with the request to know:

"I will be still and listen to the truth.
What does it mean to give and to receive?"
What does it mean to be truly gentle?

When you ask, expect an answer. Know that there is a new way for you to learn, as turning inward is where your teacher is. If you find yourself having any difficulty, simply go back to focusing on your breathing and quiet your mind. Remember, each minute spent in listening to your inner guidance is immeasurable in its worth.

LESSON EIGHT

"Truth will correct all errors in my mind."

Imagine a state of mind beyond all illusion and without fear. We have all experienced such a state, even if only for a second. Unfortunately, many of us spend the majority of our time running from one activity to the next, tense, without a true sense of purpose. We call this hectic pace "reality" and minimize or repress consciousness of other times when life seems perfectly peaceful.

Today, stop living this insanity. Recall a time—even if it was less than one minute in your whole life, even if in a dream—when there was perfect stillness and peace. Imagine this peaceful moment extending without limit, into eternity. Allow your sense of stillness to be multiplied a thousand times. This is the truth of who you are, limitless in gentleness and peace. Let yourself sit and enjoy this wonderful place.

You are one with all that is and all that will be. You are whole. Any thoughts other than these are errors, illusions of the mind that are in need of correction.

You may have thought that you needed to *do* something, or *accomplish* something, in order to experience happiness. This is not the case. Happiness is like a free-flowing stream that will run effortlessly unless dammed by fear. In other words, as long as you remain afraid, full happiness will elude you. You will not find happiness as long as you are afraid of yourself, afraid of your past, afraid of your parents, afraid of success or failure, afraid of not pleasing others, afraid of the future, afraid of not being approved of. Once fear diminishes, you will find, when you least expect it, happiness has entered your life. After years of looking, striving, achieving, and conquering, happiness enters into your life unsolicited. Love, truth, and happiness are really different words describing the same thing: the state of mind absent of fear. Today's lesson is geared towards achieving this state.

You may think that truth and purpose in life elude you. This is not so. Truth stands in the light and in the open. It never hides, it always waits. It is impossible to seek the truth about who you are and not find it. Today be positive that truth—the fearless state of oneness—will enter your life by practicing the lesson throughout the day.

You may think that you are unworthy of love and gentleness because of things that you have done in the past. This is the proclamation of the ego and has no basis in truth. Know that there is no reason that happiness is out of your reach: No matter who you are or what you may have done, you are worthy of love and gentleness.

Ask that your inner guide be in your awareness as you walk through your day. Let your inner guide lead you in everything that you do. Do not make any decisions without turning inward and quieting yourself. If you forget and find yourself off track, simply reassert your desire to follow your guidance.

Don't forget your function today. Each time that you say, with confidence and commitment, "Truth will correct all errors in my mind," you are reminding yourself that you are not separate from love. By repeating today's lesson you are affirming that love will shine through fear.

Joy

Joy is the inevitable result of gentleness.
.. The open hands of gentleness are always filled.
A Course in Miracles

Joy is the natural result of gentleness, and gentleness means that fear has subsided. Now what could possibly interfere with joy? Joy is the simple result of choosing to follow the path of gentleness. The gentle receive what they offer. For this reason they know joy.

Joy is an extension of gentleness based in the Whole Mind, as grief is an extension of attack in the Ego Mind. We are always choosing which of these cycles we prefer. Joy is a very simple experience, therefore it has a difficult time surviving in a complicated society. We have to be *alive in the moment* in order to experience joy. Unfortunately many of us have become numbed, deadened, and preoccupied with the past and the future. We believe that we must expose ourselves to endless stimuli and entertainment in order to have what are only fleeting moments of pseudo-joy.

In the past I numbed myself in every way that I could imagine. I recall as a teenager feeling that the only time I really felt "alive" was going very fast on my motorcycle. I would try to experience intimacy by means of drugs and alcoholic intoxication, thereby attaining a forced and illusionary feeling of warmth and openness. Later, as an adult, I would make efforts to enjoy a hike while preoccupied with work or other concerns. I would attempt to be authoritative and smart, adding degrees after my name, believing that status and prestige would give me joy. My thrill seeking from adolescence continued into adulthood and I began aerobatic flying. I was looking for ways of feeling keenly alive, and stakes and risks escalated. I seemed unable to find joy in simple things. Attempts to enjoy my life felt as though I were trying to suck water through a straw that had a constantly shrinking diameter. I became very thirsty, tired, and anxious. Even after a great deal of individual therapy, self-help books, and group work, I still found myself looking for ways to feel joy.

One day during a meditation I realized that if I could not experience joy sitting there, with no stimuli, all the entertainment, thrill seeking, and prestige were not going to do any good. In that moment I realized that joy is a very simple thing that can well up inside of us like a powerful geyser. If we do not know and honor the simplicity of joy we will only find emptiness in the things that we do.

Joy comes from being gentle and tender in our approach to life. This requires a certain amount of sensitivity. Unfortunately many of us were raised in homes that discouraged sensitivity and encouraged guardedness.

Ideally, to become sensitive, we need some close direction during our childhood years, some healthy guidance on how to live. Many of us did not receive this. Our direction often came from television and other forms of media. True sensitivity is developed in children who receive unconditional love and encouragement to explore both the world and themselves.

For children in school, there is constant pressure to learn, to gather information and store it in their little minds. Most educational institutions place little emphasis on knowing ourselves. Indeed, we are taught that self-knowledge "just happens." But this is not true. We need the tools that will help us come to know ourselves.

When we are shamed as children—made to feel that who we are is *bad*—we begin to withdraw from the world. We may not look like we have removed ourselves. We may be very active in the world, but we have become internally removed and guarded. With shame we lose the ability to be sensitive. Joy becomes impossible.

A pessimistic scenario? Many of us, having been shamed, have lost the ability to be sensitive. The good news is that it is never too late to become sensitive. Ask yourself honestly, *Do I want to acquire sensitivity?* Many of us equate the words sensitive and vulnerable with pain and negative experiences. No small number of us have been criticized with the words, "You're too sensitive."

It is important for you to decide what sensitivity is, and if becoming more sensitive is important to you. Study people whom you consider to be joyous. Also observe and think about those who seem to just live on the planet but do not have any real joy or purpose. Isn't the difference between these two sets of people their ability or inability to be sensitive, to be gentle and tender? Haven't we seen how the joyous are able to reach out, unguarded and without fear? Lack of sensitivity deadens us while we are alive.

Commit yourself, beginning now, to *feel* life around you. Imagine that there is a volume or intensity control dial on everything around you. You can turn it up. Being sensitive means being able to feel and experience life in the moment. This is all that you need to attend to. Be aware, and experience.

For those who may have been shamed as children, give the child within you the permission to explore the world. If you happen to have a child, as I do, let them be your teacher. Roll on the grass with them. Smell the smells and listen to the sounds. Go to the beach without a book, and *really* be at the beach. Go on a walk without a thousand thoughts in your head. Let yourself *live* life.

You may encounter painful or unwanted realities in your day-to-day activity that are very real. Allow yourself to be present to what is occurring. Don't judge or label a specific event as good or bad. When you are quick to label something or someone, you remove yourself. You become a little more desensitized.

It is important to remember that being sensitive does not mean taking on another's pain. This would constitute a lack of personal boundaries. If you see suffering, compassionately attend to it. But don't make it your own.

A few years ago I saw a stray cat get hit by a car. It was along a busy street in an affluent community during commute hour. The driver did not stop, and the cat lay by the side of the road. I was walking and was a fair distance away. As I approached I realized that no one was stopping. Their 8:00 A.M. appointments apparently took priority. When I finally arrived to where the cat lay, two other people had stopped. They suggested that somebody "call someone." They did not want to become involved in any serious manner. I ended up taking the cat to the vet, and later caring for it at home. The cat was a wonderful animal, full of personality and spunk.

When I reflect on that day, I see the epidemic emotional distance and numbness in our society. If we want joy we must become sensitive to other beings and ourselves. We must have the willingness to react *from our hearts in the moment,* rather than from our heads where we are worrying about the future.

Becoming sensitive may seem painful and unwanted. You may ask, how can I have joy if all I do is look at suffering? I had a very powerful lesson in this. Early in 1982 I had the opportunity to spend some time in India with Mother Teresa and the sisters that served with her at the Missionaries of Charity. In retrospect, I recall expecting to find the sisters depressed and "burnt out." All of them were dealing with death, suffering, and despair twenty-four hours a day. They worked with unwanted children and the poorest of the poor. Yet what I found was that Mother Teresa and the sisters were the most joyful people that I had ever been around.

I have discovered in myself, and I have observed in others, that it is easy to find fragmentation and dysfunction in people. This is what the Ego Mind tells us to do and what many of us have become accustomed to doing. We look to our spouses and see what is "wrong" with them. We look to our children and think, "If only they were brighter," or "better behaved," or "more athletic." We look to our parents and see only the negative things that they did. We look at ourselves and shovel shame into our soul by holding on to all the "bad" things that we have done in the past.

Yet there is another way of seeing ourselves and the world. At the Missionaries of Charity, I began to learn that being sensitive does not necessarily mean identifying with and taking on pain. Mother Teresa and the sisters were doing something much greater than absorbing the suffering of others. Instead, they behaved with sensitivity, acknowledging the love, dignity, and individuality of each person. This is the joy that lies *beyond* the suffering.

When we choose to listen to the quiet voice of the Whole Mind, we see beyond the surface layer of the ego's fragmentation. We see the the wholeness of the individual. This is how we begin to experience true compassion and unconditional love. This is how we find the true meaning of joy.

WHAT IS BEAUTY?

As I look out my window I see golden rolling hills studded with oak trees. In the valley below, cows chew their breakfast of alfalfa. The sun shines hazily through distant cirrus clouds. It is a very lovely scene to look out upon. It also prompts the question, "What is beauty?"

I encourage you to ask yourself this question now, because beauty and joy overlap; they share common borders. You may answer the question by describing a series of beautiful things; perhaps a fine painting, a compelling face, a child's smile, or a lovely mountain lake. If asked, perhaps any of us would say that these things are beautiful. But is this all that beauty is, or is this only the surface?

Most of us have *learned* about what we now think is beautiful. The *perception* of external beauty, at least in part, is a learned phenomenon. A thing of beauty may be a form, or a design, or even an aspect of life. You may have a favorite place to watch a sunset, lavish in color and hue. Or you may enjoy being surrounded by the plush texture and bold pattern of a handmade quilt.

A sunset, a texture, a pattern—these are all surface expressions of beauty. Yet there is something much deeper to which we must become sensitive if we are to experience the depths of joy.

Deep beauty does not lie in an external manifestation, but rather in the *internal* experience of being sensitive to all things. The *experience* of beauty is in recognizing the interconnectedness of all that we experience, with all of our senses. There is no more powerful or joyful experience than this.

When we separate what we see into categories of status—beautiful, ugly, poor, rich, pleasurable, painful—we miss the opportunity to experience joy. What really matters is to be in a state of oneness with everything. This is the experience of beauty that directly leads to the experience of joy. It is being sensitive to all things, and all aspects of life.

A house full of beautiful objects will stand empty if no love exists between the inhabitants. In the same way, it is recognition of our inner beauty that gives meaning to external form. Without being able to see your inner beauty and connection with all life, your existence will be as empty as that house filled with beautiful objects but absent of love.

I remember going into an antique shop a number of years ago where I found a beautiful Japanese kimono. Because the outside was dark grey and the brightest colors were all on the inside, I thought that the storekeeper had hung it up inside-out, and I brought this to his attention. In response, he smiled at me kindly and explained that the kimono was made with the beautiful embroidery on the inside to symbolize the inner beauty of the person who wore it.

When we come to know our inner beauty, the external

world takes on a gentle and peaceful presence. The problem with many of us is that we are too busy in our daily lives. We are preoccupied with work, worried about the future, or planning our next vacation. We miss the subtle beauty of who we are. Taking the time to gain and develop a deep appreciation of your inner beauty is a precursor to experiencing joy.

The shallow or limited mind does not look to the underlying oneness of life. It sees no importance in cultivating our inner beauty. The limited mind would have great difficulty in experiencing the overwhelming joy that comes from looking at something that is truly beautiful. From a limited mind, I may look outside my window and say that what I see is beautiful. But, from a place of unlimited depth and unity, I can experience the joy of the beauty of what I see.

WHAT IS
SPIRITUALITY AND LOVE?

A conversation on joy, beauty, and sensitivity would be incomplete without talking about spirituality and love. In my mind, spirituality does not necessarily have anything to do with religion. Spirituality is not inherent in one religion or another; it is the thread of experience at the heart of all faiths, the universal experience of oneness. In one sentence, *spirituality is the sensitivity to inner beauty, and an intimate connection with all life.*

To be a spiritual person means that you do not deny any aspect of the universe. You become sensitive to all of it: to the animal who is caged and hungry, to the laughter of children walking home from school, to the tears of a friend, to all things that surround you. It is from this sensitivity that we are truly able to experience joy and beauty. The awareness of the wholeness of your existence brings the ability to love. Without spirituality—true sensitivity—there is only surface beauty. Without spirituality, life lacks the experience of the depth of love.

Love simply exists in our hearts and is shared; it has no object. This doesn't mean that we can't love another person, but it does mean that withholding love affects our capacity to experience love. The mind that loves is a spiritual mind, because it sees no one more worthy of love than another person. Love *is.* It is not held, confined to a specific belief system, or limited in any way.

In order to experience the depth of joy we must become more sensitive to the wholeness and perfect integration of the universe, of which we are a part. Reflecting back, at one time this statement would have sounded like New Age "psychobabble" to me. Yet I have found in my psychological and spiritual studies that the underlying oneness of the universe has been spoken about for centuries in the world's great spiritual traditions. Even more remarkable, pages from a modern textbook on physics sound remarkably similar to ancient spiritual teachings. This is because scientists have been finding that all aspects of the universe are integrated, and therefore all intimately affect one another. A butterfly flapping its wings in China, for example, affects the weather in California. Nowadays, notions such as "integration" and "connectedness" are supported by empirical evidence.

I invite you to focus on joy more in your life by looking to the wholeness in yourself and others. You may begin by practicing the following lessons.

LESSON NINE

"Light and joy and peace abide in me."

When we place value in the Ego Mind we believe in guilt and shame.

When we accept the idea that we are guilty (we have done unforgivable things) and that we are shameful (who we are is "bad"), we fear that if the truth about us were known we would be abandoned. Yet we rarely question this shame, because we feel it is so intense if we looked at it we would never return to a sane life. It is a darkness that we dare not enter, for the demons would instantly overpower us.

The ego can be very convincing and effective in firmly establishing our belief in these thoughts. We do not see that shame and guilt are based on the past, that the past exists only in our mind, and that therefore our shame and guilt are based on nothing.

Today begin to learn that light, joy, and peace are who you are. Learn that you are not darkness, guilt, and shame.

Do not question the ego from the reference point of fear. This only more firmly establishes its argument. Instead, focus on the truth about yourself. Your inner beauty has been kept safe for you throughout time. It is who you are. It lies waiting for you to look upon it with eyes and heart based in the present. The fearful and shameful self that you think you created is but a dream. In truth you are one with all that is.

Your release from shame and guilt require the acceptance of only one thought: *"You are as love created you, not what you think you made of yourself."* Whatever mistakes you may have made in your life don't matter. The truth about you remains unchanged. Love is eternal and unalterable. You are, and will forever be, created in love. "Light, joy, and peace abide in you" now, because they have always been there and always will be. It is that simple.

Devote the first five minutes of every waking hour to today's lesson. Begin by closing your eyes and briefly focusing your attention towards your breathing. Then say to yourself:

> *"'Light and joy and peace abide in me.'*
> *My shamelessness is guaranteed by love."*

Next, put away all of your false self-images. When any thought that brings you anything other than light, peace, and joy enters your mind tell yourself, "This is not who I am. I made this up about myself, or believed a faulty perception that somebody else told me."

You are either love or the fearful image that your ego made. Only one self can be true; resist having a split mind. Experience the unity of all that is around you. Appreciate the love in all life. Don't interfere with the natural state of joy by hiding your inner beauty in layers of shame and guilt. Stop separating, labeling, and categorizing. As you do you will begin to see the connectedness of all life.

You may not yet be willing to use the first five minutes of every hour to practice. At a minimum remind yourself each hour:

> *"'Light and joy and peace abide in me.'*
> *My shamelessness is guaranteed by love."*

Then close your eyes and remind yourself that this is the truth about who you are. This alone will begin to plant the seeds that will later increase your commitment.

Should a situation arise that seems to be upsetting, quickly, before giving the "upset" any power, dispel the illusion of fear by repeating the lesson again. Similarly, should anger or blame towards another enter into your awareness, silently say to him/her:

> *"'Light and joy and peace abide in you.'*
> *Your shamelessness is guaranteed by love."*

Don't worry if today you don't let go of all guilt and shame. Just know that you can do a great deal to bring the idea into your mind. Today you start building a new foundation based on love.

LESSON TEN

My joy comes from being sensitive to who I am.

Today's lesson is devoted to looking for joy where it can be found. Caught up in a busy schedule, it's easy to start thinking that joy comes from outside of yourself. You may think that if you have more friends, more money, or more recognition that you will have more joy. You end up on a roller-coaster ride when you spend your energy looking to the world to make yourself joyful. If you think that others must fully approve of you, or that you must please others, you cannot experience true joy. In the ability to know who you are joy blossoms in your heart.

To have joy, to be inwardly aware, one is required to let go of the things that are not important. Essentially the unimportant is what is valueless. Joy is trusting that the light within you is who you are. The light of love and forgiveness begins to shine through all of the layers of darkness when you turn inward and become sensitive to who you are.

Celebrate yourself today. Take joy in who you are. Be thankful for the life you have and all those who come into your life to teach you the lessons you need to learn. Know there is not one person in your life who is not there to teach you, if you are willing to learn. When you see the world in this light, you will indeed see quite a different world.

Our exercises for today will be joyful and happy ones. We extend our gratitude for the passing of the old (looking to the world to make us happy) and the entering of the new (becoming sensitive to who we are). We begin with forgiveness in order to become sensitive to who we are.

Your longer practice periods (at least two fifteen-minute periods) are devoted to looking at yourself through the eyes of forgiveness. Remind yourself that forgiveness, nothing else, is your purpose is today. Know that in all of the world there is no more important task than this. Your single purpose will make your goal easy to reach. But if you have other priorities it will be difficult to achieve. When you are looking at yourself through the eyes of guilt you are hallucinating—you are actually seeing things that are not there. This is because shame and guilt are based upon the past, and the past is gone.

Begin your longer practice periods by telling yourself:

"Who I am lies beyond my belief in shame and guilt.
Forgiveness is how I can see who I am."

Do not dwell on the past today. Adopt an open mind. Wash your mind of all the ideas that you thought were true. Free yourself from all the concepts that you made about yourself. Today look upon yourself as though you were meeting yourself for the first time. You do not know who you are. Wait for who you are to be revealed in the silence of the present moment. As you wait slowly and patiently repeat to yourself:

"I have forgiven myself and all the world.
The light of love will show me the way."

Acknowledge your higher power. State that you know you can't fail because you trust it. This one statement, if you mean it, will make all the difference in how you feel. In this statement is the release from fear.

Your shorter practice periods are simply momentary reminders of your goal for the day. If you can do this every quarter of an hour or so, your joy will be greatly increased. Remember that today is a time of celebration in which you give thanks for life itself and take joy in the power of forgiveness. Know with confidence that today marks a new beginning for you.

Before going to bed read the following reminder of the day's lesson.

> *This day was dedicated to the serenity that is with*
> *you at all times. It marks a beginning in that you*
> *are forgiving yourself and are becoming sensitive to*
> *who you are. Joy is in you, and it can now be shared*
> *with others. Extend forgiveness to yourself and*
> *others and you will never be without joy. Let your*
> *dreams celebrate the beginning of your vision that*
> *has come today to replace the guilt and shame that*
> *you thought were so real.*

Defenselessness: The Attitude of Gratitude

The gentle letting go of the demands
and attachments of your mind
represents the highest level of
true strength and character in a human being.
Ken Keys, Jr. in
Prescriptions for
Happiness

Being defenseless—without judgment, neither afraid nor predicting attacks by others—is the most natural thing in the world. It is a direct reflection and acknowledgment of who we are.

The ego believes that whatever is valuable to us needs defending. Wars are a result of this belief. No one can have unwavering peace of mind until he or she fully realizes that he or she is the essence of love. Love is the one thing that needs no defense. Indeed, defense actually hides love from us.

This principle is acceptable once the belief system of the Ego Mind is seen for what it is: an ideology based on fear and rooted in the past.

When I was a child growing up in Tiburon, in Northern California, I remember an old man who lived above a tattered storefront in the town center. Peeking into the dust-caked windows of the shop below his apartment revealed stacks of pans and baking implements, and a barely visible sign that proclaimed "Morreli's Bakery."

Mr. Morreli, proprietor of the bakery as well as tenant of the apartment above it, cut a short, stodgy figure and was rarely seen without his cigar. Though he ran the bakery himself, it was seldom open. A reclusive man, Mr. Morreli kept the drapes to his upstairs apartment drawn, and the doors to his bakeshop shut up tightly with lock and key.

As a boy, the old man's life puzzled me. Why would anyone own a store that almost never opened? It was almost always locked, and full of useless, dirty items. Such questions stayed with me even after I left my parents' home and moved away.

When I finished college I moved back to my hometown. I was pleasantly surprised to hear that Mr. Morreli was still living. He had moved his always-closed bakery to a smaller location, but retained the apartment upstairs. I often thought of Mr. Morreli and wondered what his life must be like.

At the time, in the late 1970s, I happened to be renting a house from a man named John. I got to know John, and noticed that he regularly visited Mr. Morreli. John gave the old baker a great deal of loving support. I was touched by their relationship and John's commitment to help Mr. Morreli's life close in a dignified manner.

In recent years, Mr. Morreli's memory has served as a metaphor reminding me of the foolish ways I too have guarded and defended myself: How many times I noticed myself harboring a belief system that was rarely open, a heart that was bolted shut, a house full of useful trinkets I insisted were precious, and a mind full of useless and valueless thoughts.

It has been a long time now since I lived in Tiburon, and many years since Mr. Morreli passed away. Yet I still see reflections of Mr. Morreli's Bakery in the windows that now house a trendy boutique. When I look up to the windows that once had the drawn yellowing drapes, I remind myself to turn within. I ask myself if I am closed minded, whether my heart is locked. I ask myself whether I have put a lot of value in material possessions that have no value of their own. Morreli's corner is a reminder for me to let others into my life.

The most important lesson I have ever learned is: "It is not danger that comes when I lay down my defenses. It is safety. It is peace of mind. It is joy." When we finally decide to look beyond our defenses, we discover that there is nothing real to defend in the first place. We realize what has value needs no defense. As our trust increases, we become naturally less defensive.

When we begin to let go of defenses we can find humor rather than fear and pain. We see reminders of how silly we have behaved in the past. One of my most consistent reminders of how our defenses never bring us what we want is my dog, Vali. She is a Queensland Heeler and is quite intelligent. But she is also so guarded and protective that she has a hard time having fun when another dog comes to visit. I remember one instance when we had a pair of dogs over at the house: The two played together for hours, rolling in the grass and chasing one another. Vali, on the other hand, was either guarding her bed or protecting her food dish. Increasingly fearful that one of the other dogs might use her things, she was clearly not having fun in the process.

If I am honest with myself, I can see that over the years I have behaved a lot like Vali. Whenever I have chosen to be guarded instead of defenseless I have been just like her. I feared loss of some kind. It is important to recognize the thought system that lies beneath our defensive attitude and behavior.

Fear is at the core of defensiveness. Without fear you would not feel that you were in need of defense. Two important elements underlie your fear. First, you believe that fear is involuntary, and you think it is out of your control. Second, you believe that the object of your fear is real.

Fear will continue as long as these two beliefs remain intact, and therefore so will defensive behavior. Resolving conflict and letting fear go will help in adopting an attitude of defenselessness. This, in turn, will bring you peace of mind and enhance your personal relationships.

FEAR AND CONFLICT

Fear prevents you from being able to listen to your inner guidance. Yet fear is under your control because fear is merely a result of what you think. Like so many people, you may believe that you are responsible for what you *do*, but not for what you *think*. But, "the truth is that you are responsible for what you think, because it is only at this level that you can exercise choice."

Behavior simply follows thought. In this way, defensiveness simply follows fear. Being responsible for our thinking may sound like a heavy burden, but there is nothing more singularly powerful than reclaiming and developing the power of thought.

Behavior is a symptom of an underlying thought. As such, I feel that any therapy or path to growth that only changes behavior is incomplete. It is true that behavioral change can occur by reinforcing or punishing the behavior and never addressing the thought or subjective experience that is beneath. In some cases, quite profound behavioral change can be made without ever addressing the level of thought. Yet this does not speak to the individual's inner *subjective* experience.

If peace of mind is to be yours, you must change your mind, not just your behavior. This most definitely requires a deep willingness and desire. Fear is always a sign that you are feeling (and therefore believing) that you are separate from others. Wherever there is the belief in separation there is fear. Conversely, whenever there is the recognition of our underlying oneness, there is peace of mind.

Fear arises when you have not made up your mind about who you are and what you want. The ego functions in split goals, and the result is always fear. With two opposing thoughts, the mind is caught in a type of double-bind. I may be certain, for example, that acquiring a new house will make me happy, yet also not be sure that I can afford it. As a result of this belief, I might buy a house and worry constantly about the payments, or not buy the house and go through my daily life certain that I will never be happy.

Remember that only your mind can produce fear. The main way it does so is by having two conflicting goals or thoughts. This dilemma can be remedied only by accepting a unifying goal of the whole mind. Below you will find examples of split-thoughts and split-goals of the Ego Mind, and unifying goals of the Whole Mind. The results of fear or peace of mind are readily apparent.

EXAMPLES OF
CONFLICTING GOALS / BELIEFS
OF THE EGO MIND

1. a. I want to be self-confident and successful.
   b. If people see me for who I am I will not be accepted.

2. a. To be a good person I must have strong moral values.
   b. I have done things that are unforgivable.

3. a. I want to love and be loved.
   b. I should beware of being hurt at all times.

4. a. I want to feel close to others.
   b. I should judge others and be sure not to miss anything.

5. a. I want to be happy and whole.
   b. I need the approval of others.

EXAMPLES OF
UNIFYING GOALS OF THE WHOLE MIND

1. My goal is to accept rather than judge others.
2. My goal is to release myself from the bondage of the past.
3. My goal is to focus on healing rather than hurting.
4. My goal is to forgive myself and others.
5. My goal is to know all that love offers and to do this by offering love.

WHO WE ARE IN TRUTH
NEEDS NO DEFENSE

*Fear arises when you have not made up your mind
about who you are or what you want.*

When we become defensive we are accepting a fear-based reality that tells us that we are in constant danger. If we do not question the foundation that this fear rests upon, we will never find peace of mind. We will continue to build elaborate defenses. I believe that there are two fundamental aspects of who we are that must be embraced if we are to move beyond the fear of the Ego Mind. Namely:

1. *Who we are is love.* Love is our natural inheritance and the truth about who we are.
   Love never abandons us, *it is we who can
   choose to abandon it.* We abandon love when
   we cover it with cloaks of guilt and shame.
   Once covered, we can choose to believe
   that love has disappeared and that guilt and
   shame are who we are. Yet, as any child
   learns, when something is covered we need
   only to lift the cover and what is beneath
   will reappear.

2. *What every human being wants is to experience
   love, kindness, and union.* Beyond all other
   little goals and achievements we may have
   in life, this yearning is in our hearts and
   minds when we arrive into this world and
   when we depart from it.

Believe in these two principles and you will no longer deceive yourself that you need to live in fear and constantly defend yourself. When you are defensive you close the door to the opportunity to be aware of love. By the mere fact that you are being defensive, you are believing in fear.

It may seem like adopting an attitude of defenselessness would be crazy in the world today. You may look around you and see an image of the world that demands defenses for your mere survival.

"There is another way of looking at the world." If you are to ever experience consistent peace of mind, you must begin to adopt it. The two principles of love described above teach us that regardless of what a person's behavior is, what he or she is really asking for is love.

Unfortunately, most people in our society are taught to adopt a fear-based attitude at a very early age: For good reason, children are told to be careful of strangers. The television broadcasts murders and kidnapings. Indeed, there are many more "Be afraid!" warnings in our society than there are messages that tell us, "You are safe and secure."

As a psychologist spending time with troubled youth, I have seen some very elaborate defense systems. The increase in teen suicide and pregnancy, as well as unsafe schools, drug use, and gang activity is evidence of this. I have asked myself what these young people must believe about themselves and the world to be behaving in isolating, rageful, rebellious, and dishonest ways. As a therapist, to be of any help at all, I have to be willing to explore with them their inner and subjective lives that they have kept so well guarded.

Seven years ago, Paul and Carol Applegate came to see me. They were the concerned and confused parents of Rick, a troubled sixteen-year-old. Rick had been caught using marijuana and had been lying about the fact he had been skipping school. Before five minutes of our session had elapsed, I realized Paul and Carol were clearly in a great deal of emotional pain, which revealed itself in several different ways.

Paul, a tall man with slightly graying hair, appeared mildly out of place in his business suit. I couldn't help but wonder if he wore it to the session to reassure himself of his own authority, as he clearly felt none with his son. Carol sat sobbing as her husband distantly and matter-of-factly told me of their problems with Rick. The more Paul spoke, the deeper Carol sunk into her chair, as though she wanted to disappear into the pattern of the fabric. There was not an accusatory tone in Paul's voice—indeed his voice resembled that of a newscaster telling of yet another tragedy—but it was clear that they both believed Carol was to blame for Rick's behavior. Perhaps, at the time, they thought that *someone* had to be blamed. Possessing little self-esteem, Carol covertly volunteered, as she probably had most her life.

As the session continued a picture of their son Rick began to emerge. Apparently the young man had been a "model child" until entering high school. An only child, Rick served as the center of Carol's life for many years. As the boy became a teenager, however, he began distancing himself from his mother. Carol clearly thought that she was losing the only companion she had.

Due to his professional responsibilities, Rick's father was away a great deal of the time. In fact, Paul spent less and less time with his family as the years went on. During our session, Paul repeatedly emphasized his responsibilities to the family; for him, responsibilities meant that he had to make a certain amount of money. And although Paul plainly loved his son, he did so from such emotional distance that Rick could never know this.

Paul was not sure how, or where, to even when to begin with Rick's current problems. As a result of not wanting to feel or appear incompetent, Paul showed no emotion whatsoever during the first session. In the second session, however, Paul became angry when he began to discuss how his son had been defying his "orders."

Rick was experimenting with marijuana, though it did not yet appear that he was chemically dependent. Neither parent consumed alcohol or other drugs, but Paul had grown up in an alcoholic home. Also, neither Paul nor Carol were able to communicate much about their feelings, even though both were clearly in emotional pain.

It was clear to me after a few sessions that Rick was acting out in a variety of ways that reflected problems in the family. Family therapy was needed. Both parents seemed surprised when I suggested this, and seemed to think that this meant they had been "bad" parents. They would have preferred it if I had simply asked them to bring Rick in to be "fixed" then returned their son as soon as he was "back to normal."

I explained to them that families work as a system, and that one member will often manifest the problems that underlie family conflict. For change to occur, every member must grow. In this particular family, the first obstacle to overcome would be the belief that there has to be someone to blame. With this idea understood, the emphasis could be on growth, not fault.

Initially, sixteen-year-old Rick was a reluctant participant in therapy. Whenever he spent time with his parents, he anticipated criticism. As time went on, he was able to begin talking about his real feelings—anger, hurt, fear, and anguish—rather than merely continuing his defensive and distancing behavior.

Though both parents loved Rick very much, they had some problems in parenting. Paul would criticize and control, and rarely expressed his love in positive ways. Carol tended to feel powerless, and never offered any limits or direction. Many of these problems stemmed from their families of origin.

As the therapy progressed it became clear that Paul felt competent and confident at work, but inadequate and awkward in his role as a father. Not surprisingly, Rick felt that his father didn't really like him. With financial matters, his highest priority, Paul had continued to distance himself from his son. Rick had been hurt by his father's continued distancing. Unable to speak of the hurt, Rick began to act out. Slowly they were both able to let their feelings be known. As time went on they were able to be more present and genuine with one another, both during the sessions, and at home.

Carol and Paul had never given much thought to their relationship, and simply continued on a "tread mill" in the marriage. For the first time, with therapy, they were able to explore their relationship, and themselves, with some depth. Each of them began to be able to get beyond blame. This also had an effect upon Rick, for he had never really seen his parents relate on an emotional level. Up to then, he had no role models on how to effectively communicate feelings.

Carol began to be more assertive in the relationship with her husband, and within the family context in general. Rick previously had little respect for his mother, because he felt that she was everyone's doormat. Because he had seen so many people treat her poorly, including Paul, Rick did so too. Indeed, he would rage at his mother at the drop of a hat. Through therapy, Rick began to learn how to discuss his feelings, and so became better able to reveal his anger in an effective way.

In short, the family members had all been defensive in their thinking and behavior, though previously, only Rick's stood out. Each person needed to identify and work through his or her own fears and defenses.

There is a three-step process similar to the one the Applegates used that you can use to identify and change your defensive behavior.

First, identify the defensive thought or belief that you harbor, and also the resulting behavior. Remember that there is never a behavior that is not preceded by some belief. Fear-based beliefs always lead to defensive behavior and feelings of isolation. This step requires you to find the thought or belief that creates feelings of separation rather than closeness.

Second, identify what it is that you really want. Ultimately, this will always be some aspect of love.

Third, identify what alternative belief or attitude and coinciding behavior you would like to adopt in order to experience the results you wish.

In regard to the Applegate family, these steps can be summarized as follows:

RICK

1. Rick believed that he was not a good person because he was not liked by his father. He also believed that his mother was incapable of providing clear boundaries and limits. Having low self-esteem and no boundaries, Rick began to act out. Raging, lying, and using drugs became commonplace.
2. What Rick really wanted was to feel acceptance and unconditional love. He wanted his father to be approachable. He wanted to know that his mother could assert herself and provide limits for him. (As most teenagers, Rick often stated he wanted unlimited freedom. Yet Rick needed some firm limits.)
3. Rick began to believe that he was worthwhile and that he could communicate his feelings. As he was able to talk to his parents more, and as they were able to really listen, his self-esteem increased.

PAUL

1. On the surface, Paul believed that a father's job was to provide financial security. He thought feelings should be known without having to talk about them. But on a deeper level, Paul had always longed for a relationship with his own father. Because he never experienced feelings being expressed in his family of origin, he had no idea how to express his love for his own son. Feeling completely unable to reach his son, Paul believed that he was inadequate. To defend

against feelings of inadequacy he became increasingly distant. Paul adopted the role of "good provider" to compensate for underlying low self-esteem.

2. What Paul really wanted was to feel deep intimacy with his family. He yearned to be genuinely present with his son and wife.

3. Paul began to explore and resolve his family of origin issues. As he did he was able to value being unguarded and genuine. He wanted nothing more than to know himself and to share himself without shame or guilt.

CAROL

1. Carol believed that she was the cause of any negative situation that surfaced in the family. Her defense was to accept blame without question. This ensured that she had at least some role in life, even though she never felt good about herself.

2. Carol wanted support, recognition, and acceptance. She did not want blame for all of life's problems.

3. Carol began to believe that she was not responsible for other people's happiness. Freedom came as she accepted responsibility for her own feelings. This realization allowed her to be more compassionate and assertive.

LESSON ELEVEN

"Love is the way I walk in gratitude."

From the ego's belief in fear comes guardedness, defensiveness, emotional isolation, and all forms of attack. They are self-perpetuating.

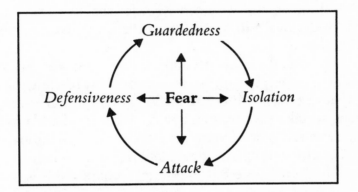

Openness, defenselessness, authenticity, and kindness come from the Whole Mind's recognition of who you are: love. They are also self-perpetuating.

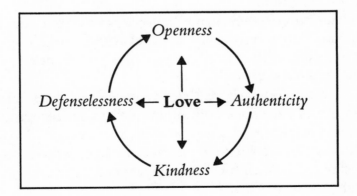

The attitude of gratitude is impossible to adopt when you believe that you are a victim of the world. With such a victim mentality, a posture of constant and rigid defense will surely follow. When we look upon the world in such a way, comfort with ourselves is impossible. The ego believes that comfort is feeling that we are better off than others. Yet how can we be truly happy when the measure of success is whether someone else suffers more than you do? If we feel good because someone is not as well off, or we have "made it to the top" at another person's expense, think again. How can we offer thanks because of suffering? 'Today walk in gratitude to the one force that ends all suffering: love.'

Individual arguments and international wars are started and maintained because one perceives an enemy battling for something that one has. We create an image of an evil enemy that threatens to take joy away and replace it with the blackness of despair. The thought of vengeance takes over. We embark on a plan to conquer our enemy, never looking at ourselves.

How can there be "winning" where there is no love? How can there be joy where there is fear? Today explore the power of love. See the lessons of love everywhere and in everything—even in situations that you don't like or don't see an immediate purpose in. You will not have to try to have gratitude, it will simply grow. Know that love makes no comparisons, and asks no one to suffer.

Seeing ourselves as not being separate from others creates an outlook of gratitude for each and every living thing. If we do not extend gratitude to all life we fail to see the beauty of our interconnectedness with all that is.

All the comparisons that you have made between yourself and others have done nothing but delay your recognition of love. *Hatred does not exist when comparisons are laid aside.* Do not be tempted to compare yourself with another in order to determine if you should be thankful. Lay comparisons aside and 'walk in gratitude, the way of love.'

It is not useful to repress anger. It is not beneficial to deny love. With a loving attitude you can allow anger to come up and quickly let it go. Know today that you have been given everything you need in order to experience love right now. This includes the ability to let go of anger. You can deny this and choose to give energy to anger, malice, and revenge. Yet you can just as easily choose to have gratitude become the single thought that replaces these insane perceptions.

Gratitude and love occupy the same mind. Similarly, anger and fear go hand in hand. Gratitude is simply an aspect of love. It is a doorway that allows love to enter into our lives. With the attitude of gratitude, joy comes in the world.

Today remind yourself many times to be grateful, and witness the changes that occur.

LESSON TWELVE

"It can be but my gratitude I earn."

This is the second step in releasing your mind from the bondage of fear and defensiveness. Most of us have become accustomed to looking to external gratification, support, thanks, and validation. This is a habit that must be given up before we can find peace of mind.

You may make attempts at being compassionate, kind, and forgiving. You may find yourself turning to attack again when you don't find people responding in the ways you expected.

Now it is time to understand that it is only *your* gratitude that matters. There are some simple facts that you will do well in recognizing today:

1. Deny your strength (internal gratitude), and weakness (searching for external validation) will become your idea of where happiness is.
2. If you see yourself as bound, bars will become your home.

3. Freedom is impossible as long as you believe
   in guilt. Gratitude and love are linked together
   in the same way that shame and fear are.

Today take time to fill your heart with gratitude for who
you are. If you have difficulty doing this it is probably because
you are holding on to the past. In so doing you believe there
are things that you should be guilty about. Today be concerned
with who you *are* (present orientation), not what you have or have
not *done* (past orientation). You may find it helpful to begin by
being grateful for your capacity to be kind to another living
being. Is this not a precious and beautiful gift that is always
available to you?

As your feelings of gratitude grow, allow your awareness
to expand to all the people in your life. Even those with whom
we are most tempted to become defensive are here to teach us
how to choose another way of being.

When you are defensive and afraid,
you have nothing.
When you have a grateful heart,
you have everything.

You may think that lack of positive response to your
gifts of compassion and gratitude means the gifts were not received. Because an individual's behavior has not changed you
may believe that they go unaffected. At such times you may be
tempted to revert back to anger, attack, and defense. Remember
that it does not matter if somebody finds your gifts unworthy.
There is some part of their mind that joins with yours in gratitude. No kind thought goes unnoticed.

Even with those who you love, perhaps your spouse and
children, you are probably tempted to withdraw your gifts of
kindness. You trade them for blame and guilt. Today make an
effort to not do this, for such behavior never gives you peace.

Give thanks to your higher power for guiding your life. Be thankful for love itself. Gratitude is a part of love, and the experience of love is all that your higher power is concerned with. Follow your guidance and all gratitude is yours. What can be more pure than following the path that love lays before you?

Extend kindness,
and be thankful your heart is full.
Forgive,
and be grateful that you are forgiven.
Love,
and receive your gift as you give it.
Have gratitude,
and you are complete.

Generosity

Even if we knew a thousand times more
of ourselves, we would never reach bottom.
We would still remain an enigma to ourselves,
as our fellow man would remain an enigma to us.
The only way to full knowledge lies
in the act of love:
this act transcends thought, it transcends words.
            Erich Fromm in
            The Art of Loving

Generosity is a familiar word, yet the meaning of the term deepens and expands as we develop trust. In growing up, many of us learn that the world is a place where we guard what we have acquired. 'With such a world view, generosity comes to mean "giving away" in the sense of losing something.' In our society, giving away is equated with having less. Who would opt to do so? With such a perspective, we can only be "generous" when we know what is in it for us.

In the Whole Mind, on the other hand, generosity is an extension of the ability to trust. Generosity is an attitude that is based on abundance, the knowledge that we have all we need in order to love. 'We give away in order to keep.' As you know, this concept has been emphasized throughout this book, yet it is more difficult to fully accept than any other. What makes it so difficult? It may be because it represents the obvious reversal of what many of us have learned. Here we see it in the clearest way: In regard to generosity, the Ego Mind and the Whole Mind mean the exact opposite message. Review the following.

THE EGO MIND AND GENEROSITY

1. Compare how much you have and how much others have. If you can "afford" it, give something away. Only do so if you can either look good or get something back.
2. When you give, have a clear idea of what you will get in return. Be concerned with when you will get it.
3. Use generosity as a tool of manipulation to get you want.
4. Always be concerned with having "enough." Always raise your standards when you get what you previously thought was enough.
5. Be aware that there isn't enough of what you need.
6. If somebody else has more you should be envious and jealous. Try to catch up. Take something away from them to equal the score.
7. Never be generous with those you don't like.

8. Power comes from having more than others.
9. In order to afford generosity you must constantly achieve and accumulate.
10. Don't be too generous because then other people will expect things from you.

THE WHOLE MIND
AND GENEROSITY

1. Lay comparisons aside. What is of value increases as you give it away.
2. Giving, without attachment, guarantees peace.
3. Be generous for the sake of giving. This is how you will receive.
4. Having enough is our natural state.
5. There is an endless supply of what you want (love).
6. Nobody can really have more love than another, though some can be blind to what they have.
7. Withholding generosity from another is to withhold it from yourself.
8. Power comes from seeing your interconnectedness and commonality with others.
9. In order to be generous I need do nothing other than recognize the truth about who I am.
10. Generosity is not an act, but is rather an attitude.

In my own personal experience, I have learned of generosity in many places, from many people.

While on an around-the-world trip in 1982, I had the rare opportunity of spending twenty consecutive hours with Mother Teresa. Much of this time was traveling by car through the interior of India, while some was listening to her address different groups and individuals. I felt blessed being side by side for so long with her, and took the opportunity to ask her a variety of questions that were important to me. Somehow all of her answers had the ingredient of generosity, even if she was not speaking directly about giving.

> *"Yesterday is gone. Tomorrow has not yet come.*
> *And so we have only today to make*
> *something beautiful for God."*

This was Mother Teresa's response to my question: What do you think of the future of society and the world? Walking from the poverty-infested streets of Bombay, India, and into one of Mother Teresa's Missions of Charity, I came to know "something beautiful for God." It is not that death, leprosy, and starvation don't exist inside the Mission's walls; it is the added ingredient of love and unconditional generosity that fills the hearts of all involved, transforming the atmosphere to one of hope, dignity, and compassion.

The following are further excerpts from our conversations. So that the reader can get the flavor of the time I spent with her, I have taken the liberty to thread together some of the topics. In spots I paraphrase her. I think her words clearly and directly say what generosity is. Sometimes you will see the word "God" used by Mother Teresa. If you have difficulty with such terminology, I encourage you to simply shift it to a more comfortable phrase, such as "higher power" or "inner guidance."

MOTHER TERESA
SPEAKS ON GENEROSITY

If we have a clean heart we can see, we can understand, and we can accept each other in the gift of love. The same love that created you created me, and that man dying in the streets. Before we left this morning two people died. They were picked up off of the streets in Bombay and were brought to our home. They died, but they died knowing of the love that we now talk about.

One of the men had leprosy and was starving. After giving him tender love and care, he looked up to the sister and said, "I'm going home to God." And he shut his eyes and died: very peaceful, where hours before he had been in the street.

We must be able to bring our lives to a oneness with the love that abounds in us. And to be able to do this we need a clean heart. We all have the gift of love and it is to be shared. It is a gift and we must use it to increase love and compassion. We must give up our desire to destroy. Instead we must begin to help each other. We must transform love beyond words and show it through our actions.

I will never forget some time ago in Calcutta when we didn't have sufficient food for the children. A little four-year-old child in the city, a Hindu child, heard, "Mother Teresa has no sugar." This child went home to his parents and said, "I do not want sugar for three days. I will give my sugar to Mother Teresa." It was so little, what he brought after three days, but it was real love, real generosity.

What is our purpose? It is to help each other to know, to hear, and to love. We are here to exchange the means and ways of love. Let us put this love into action. Let us know love begins at home.

Today it is as though people have no time for one another—not even their own children. They have no time to smile at each other. Let us bring back love and generosity into our lives, into our families. It is very important for us to remember to have a life of peace, of joy, of loving. And we must remember that there is no greater science than the science of love. We must learn like that little child, *it is not how much we give but how much love we put in the giving.*

After I received the Nobel Peace Prize many people came and offered their faith, offerings such as clothes and food. I remember a beggar in the street came up to me and said, "Mother

Teresa, everybody's giving to you. I also want to give. I would like to give to you all the money I have been given today." I can't tell you the joy, the radiant joy on his face because I accepted that from him. The peace of love in his face I can't express to you. I can tell you one thing. Accepting what he offered was a much greater gift than the Nobel Prize. He gave all that he had and gave it in love.

Let us try to put our love into that kind of action.

I will never forget a time in the streets of London. I took the hand of someone sitting alone in the street. He took my hand too, and said that it had been many years since someone had held his hand. So many years since he had felt the human love, the warmth of a hand. And yet hundreds of people pass by him everyday. We pass by and we pass by. Maybe in our own home we can begin, maybe today. Maybe somebody there needs love.

Let us keep the joy of loving going in our hearts. Share this joy with all beings, especially people at home with us. Love begins at home. Come home. Those close to us need our love. Our children need our tenderness, appreciation, a gentle embrace. So let us wait no longer. Let us bring this love to one another. We don't need bombs and other defenses in order to bring peace. We need tender love and compassion and the sharing of joy that comes naturally from loving one another.

It is unlikely for us to be full of attention to love all of the time. But what is very important is that we be full of *intention*. That we want to love, that we want to be generous, that we want to listen, that we want to accept our guidance, that we want to give whatever it takes with joy. This is intention. It is very important. We are precious and we are loved tenderly.

You must respect all that you do in understanding love. If you really understand love, you are ready to give that love. The demonstration that you understand love is that you share love with everyone. Nowadays people are using the brain too much. Loving is done from the heart. When you are only using your brain in trying to understand love you may get answers to many questions, and even be able to teach many high things. But if it doesn't penetrate the heart, if it is not coming from the heart to the heart, you can do very little to fully understand love. With only the brain you are inclined to forget. But something that comes from one heart to another heart, it will remain there because it is in the silence of the heart that God speaks. It is from the fullness of the heart that we may fully give and receive. Listening is the beginning. We need to listen in silence and connect the heart with the mind. This is much more penetrating than just listening with our brain.

It is easy for us to get caught up in the brain. How clever our thoughts can be, how deceiving their explanations. Our thoughts alone don't penetrate the soul. That is why we need—it doesn't matter who you are—to be alone with God to be able to accept and give. Faith is very important. If I believe, that's the beginning of love, is it not? The fruit of faith is always love, always. When I really love then I can put this love into service.

I left the Missions of Charity with two expressions of Mother Teresa's wisdom that stay with me daily:

> *Listen from the silence of the heart,*
> *speak from the fullness of the heart.*

> *The joy of loving is always between two.*
> *It begins with two, and grows from there.*

LESSON THIRTEEN

"To give and to receive are one in truth."

The truly generous realize that there is no division between giving and receiving. There is no fear because they know that whatever is truly worth having increases when given away. The generous have a state of mind so unified, darkness cannot be perceived.

The Ego Mind sees everything in terms of opposites.

This part of your mind will try to convince you that giving and receiving are opposite to one another. Today, allow opposites to crumble. In their dust find oneness and truth.

Most everyone has had the experience of giving and feeling a fullness and peace in the moment. Perhaps going out of our way for our children or spouse, lending a hand to a neighbor, or donating to a cause we believe in. These small gestures whisper a truth to us: To give is to receive.

Giving and receiving are different facets of the same thought and act. Both occur together. In understanding this principle, peace of mind and tranquility can be found. It is with this thought that we stop giving to get, stop performing to seek approval.

One thought can bring unification to all of our thinking. In perceiving the unification of giving and receiving, healing begins. Learning that "giving and receiving are the same" is very useful because it can be easily tested and applied. The positive results can speak for themselves.

Today you will find that to give is to receive. Regardless of the mood that you find yourself in, attempt to offer compassion to everyone—even those whom you may be angry at—and see how quickly peace enters into your mind. A new way of seeing yourself and the world will emerge as you focus your attention on giving and receiving compassion.

Begin the practice period today with saying to yourself:

"To give and to receive are one in truth.
I will receive what I am giving now."

Allow your eyes to gently close. For five minutes think of what you would offer everyone, to have it for yourself. For example, you might say:

"To everyone I offer quietness."
"To everyone I offer peace of mind."
"To everyone I offer gentleness."

Say each gift slowly to yourself and then pause for a while. Expect to receive the gift that you just offered. You will receive what you gave, in the exact amount in which you offered it. If you prefer, you may focus your attention on one individual to give your gifts. Know that he or she simply represents the others. Be sure not to intentionally withhold your gifts from any individual, for you surely do not want to withhold them from yourself.

Today's lesson is very simple and straightforward. It is also empirical. You can see and experience the direct results. Know that the exercises for today are designed for you to make quick advances in your learning. Your progress can only become impeded by your old habit of seeing things as opposites. Say to yourself often: "To give and to receive are one in truth."

LESSON FOURTEEN

"Truth will correct all errors in my mind."

The only thing that can correct our illusions is an experience of the truth. Errors in our thinking are only illusions that go unchallenged and unrecognized for what they really are. Yet these errors vanish with an experience of oneness. The power of the experience replaces the illusion. Where there is an experience of oneness through the act of generosity, there can not simultaneously be fear and separation.

An obstacle that we face is that our ego tells us oneness and unity mean nothing. The ego says that we are in need of defense, and nobody can be trusted. Many of us have forgotten ever having had an experience of unity. We cannot remember a time when all we were aware of was love and connection. Today we choose to give power to the truth by reversing the ego's way of thinking. Today we maximize oneness and minimize separation. We do this through realizing that generosity is the most powerful of attitudes.

Imagine what a state of mind without separation, fear, and worry would be like. How would it feel? How would you look upon yourself and others? Try to recall a time, even if it is of the faintest memory, when there was nothing in your thoughts to interrupt your peace of mind. Maybe it was only for a minute, and perhaps a very long time ago. But it was a time when you knew you were loved and were safe. Next, imagine that moment being expanded to the end of time. Allow the peace to expand and multiply with each second that passes. Lastly, think how lovely it would be for every being on the planet to be able to remember the truth about who they are. You can either contribute to their memory, or you can choose to reinforce their belief in separation. *You are making this decision with every person that you meet.*

The experience of peace that results from doing this shows us just a glimmer of the truth. With generosity there can be no fear, no doubt, no defense, and no attack. With generosity all pain of loss is over because we realize that we can always choose to give and receive in each moment. Truth is like light. Once it comes into your mind it expands everywhere. All dark thoughts of the ego vanish when we focus on generosity and unity. We become liberated from all beliefs that ever lead to conflict and distance.

In the Ego Mind love is something that comes and goes. To the ego, love can never be counted upon. In contrast, generosity of the Whole Mind does not disappear or suddenly change into something else. With generosity comes a love that does not wane in the face of pain.

In the Ego Mind, if we give a gift and determine that it is unappreciated, we then turn to attack and defense as a recourse. In the Whole Mind we see that truth needs no defense. Attack becomes impossible. Once we discover the oneness that generosity rests upon, we recognize that in taking our gifts back, we would be keeping them from ourselves.

You may think that the experience of peace is elusive and is constantly escaping your grasp. Through generosity you can begin to see that peace has lain in waiting for you, beyond time, in the eternal moment. It is impossible for anyone to truly seek oneness and not find it. Oneness is the truth that lies beneath and beyond the illusion of separation. When you ask for peace of mind you are not asking for something that you do not have; you are merely asking to recognize what is already there. Be certain that you can be generous because you already have everything to give. Begin by saying to yourself:

> *"I trust the attitude of generosity. I walk with*
> *the truth today. I count upon it entering into*
> *every minute of the day."*

Be sure when you say "Truth will correct all errors in my mind," that you know what is the truth and what is an error:

Error: I am separate. I need to constantly defend what I have. I should be more concerned with getting then giving.

Truth: I am deeply connected with all that is and all that ever will be. Love, compassion, and kindness are always in my heart. They increase when they are given away.

Today, focus on the truth. Let all errors fall to dust and be blown away by the gentle breeze of generosity. Know that to be generous means to be tolerant towards all people. All the other traits we have discussed are contained in the attitude and acts of generosity. When you can truly say, "I am generous," you are saying that you are kind, loving, trusting, and patient.

Patience

Those who are certain of the outcome can
afford to wait, and wait without anxiety . . .
the time will be as right as is the answer. And this
is true for everything that happens now
or in the future.

A Course in Miracles

Patience is the attitude we assume when we trust that everything happens at the right moment, and that we can learn from all situations. Patience really means that we have confidence in the unfolding of our life. Those who are patient trust their inner guidance.

Many of us adhere to irrational weekly schedules and timetables, but we do not recognize the irrationality. We run from task to task, person to person, place to place, as quickly as possible. We always think about what is next. We believe that controlling our environment, other people, and social situations brings us peace of mind. We become very upset when things do not go according to *our* plan.

Most of our environmental problems, many international conflicts, and all inner and interpersonal stress is born of a lack of true patience. Our forests are being depleted and our landfills are overflowing. Our "I want it all now, and do not want to be inconvenienced" attitude is destroying the planet. We walk around with high blood pressure every day throughout our workday lives, barely having time for our families. Tellingly, as they consider going to war, world leaders issue such statements as, "I've had it." Sadly, they believe violence will give them what they want in a more prompt fashion than dialog.

Wouldn't it be far more rational to live moment to moment, doing one thing at a time? Doesn't it make more sense to live lightly on the planet and not consume more than we have?

Wouldn't it be more peaceful to accept than to control, to assist rather than dominate? When you see that every occurrence in your life has the capability to teach you more deeply about love and trust, you can afford to be free of anxiety and frustration.

To be truly patient can be very difficult if your goal is always to control and never to accept. In discovering patience, it is helpful to address three different aspects of that trait: patience and its relationship to time, life situations, and people.

PATIENCE AND TIME—
THE PARADOX OF PATIENCE

Did you ever really wonder why you become impatient? Is it possibly because you are afraid? If so, what is it that you might be afraid of? Is it because you fear the future will not be as you think it should be? Or, perhaps even more so, are you afraid the past will repeat itself? Fear and impatience are connected. Similarly, trust and patience are joined.

When you believe in the rigid reality of linear time—the reality of past and future—you are bound to be very fearful. Fearful people are very impatient.

Guilt and shame are the outcome and the preservers of the belief in linear time. Together they create fears of abandonment. They create a fear that retaliation will result for what we have done, which ensures that the future will be anything but peaceful. The ego uses this damaging cycle to convince us that we cannot escape from time, guilt, and shame.

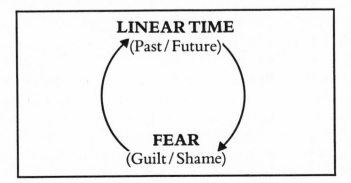

LINEAR TIME
(Past / Future)

FEAR
(Guilt / Shame)

The Whole Mind offers you the peace of the eternal moment in exchange for the fearful future you have created. In making such an exchange you are shifting your focus away from the past and the future, and towards the present moment. In so doing you begin to exchange guilt for joy, shame for love, and conflict for peace.

I have battled constantly with time during much of my life. There have seemed to be endless deadlines and a long list of expectations about what I should do with my life. Some have been self-imposed, others externally imposed. In the past, almost anything that delayed me from what *I thought* I was supposed to be doing was a source of great impatience. For example, if I found myself sitting in traffic that I had not expected, peace of mind would be quickly exchanged for a tightening of my stomach and a clenching of my fists. I would curse who was in front of me if they were not driving exactly how I thought they should be. In recent years we have witnessed this attitude taken to an extreme with people actually shooting each other on the Los Angeles freeways. Such acts epitomize the irrationality of impatience.

Until a few years ago my impatience and fight with time emerged in full force whenever I would have to wait for people who were late. Growing up I saw my parents on opposite sides of the fence when it came to leaving someplace on time. Departing on a vacation was always an eventful experience, especially if there was an airplane departure involved. My father was always ready at least an hour before we needed to leave. He usually began pacing and wringing his hands. In contrast, my mother was usually running late. This combination did not make for a relaxed departure; both approaches were dysfunctional. It is equally irrational to be rushing despite having plenty of time as it is to be always late. As an adult I seemed to unconsciously adopt my father's form of irrationality over my mother's. I found myself very impatient when anything having to do with time would arise. I feel that being on time is a good quality. But if one loses peace of mind in the process it is hardly beneficial.

When I am running behind I am still tempted to get upset. However, more often than not I am able to look at what is in front of me. I more easily let go of obsessing when I know that I am not going to make it to where I think I am supposed to be. A helpful prayer from *A Course in Miracles* is:

> *I am here only to be truly helpful.*
> *I am here to represent Him Who sent me.*
> *I do not have to worry about what to say or what to*
>   *do, because He Who sent me will direct me.*
> *I am content to be wherever He wishes,*
>   *knowing He goes there with me.*
> *I will be healed as I let Him teach me to heal.*

Living in a small town in rural Mexico taught me a lot about the purpose of time. As you might expect, in that kind of region, not everyone is on the fast track as we are in American society. Over and over again in Barra De Navidad, I found that things didn't happen at the speed *I thought* that they were supposed to. From the onset, I felt very frustrated and impatient with many of the inconveniences. Something simple like making a phone call or acquiring money from a bank sometimes took an entire day.

My purpose in living in Mexico was to discover more peace of mind. But as you can imagine, by becoming anxious when things did not happen in a timely fashion, I was anything other than peaceful. Until about ten years ago, my narcissism and grandiosity would have prompted me to react in one of these ways: I would have tried to get preferential treatment, convincing myself that *I* should not have to wait like everyone else; I would have lied, perhaps making up some sort of crisis; I would convince someone that I *immediately* had to have what I wanted; I would become manipulative and dishonest; I would have left, deeming their way incompetent and wrong; I would feel superior, but hardly happy.

But by this time in my life, I was intent on change. While in Mexico I began to realize that there must be another way to approach life's frustrations. I began to relax more and see that every situation had something to offer me. Trying to manipulate the outcome made me blind to these gifts. Slowly I was learning to *be with myself and people* rather than trying to *control time*. One particular instance stands out.

At the time I was living in Mexico, I had an old Volkswagen camper that I paid five hundred dollars for. I use to joke that I had a suntan from the knees down because I spent so much time under that van trying to fix it. Once, after being unsuccessful in repairing it, I took the camper to a shop in a very small outlying village to be worked on. The "shop" consisted of a palm-leaf lean-to and a couple of rusty chairs. Initially, I began to get frustrated. Nobody seemed to know much more than I did about the motor, and that wasn't much. Three men working on the vehicle were merely doing the same things that I had already tried.

But this time I made a real effort to put a hold on my escalating frustration. Instead, I literally changed my mind. I consciously decided that I was there for a purpose other than just to get my car repaired. I decided not to try to speed things up, or think of how much more fun I would be having if I were on the beach. In the end the "small repair" took most of two days. Instead of faceless service workers, the men working on the car became my friends.

There is no grand conclusion to the story. My purpose was much simpler and less dramatic. Experientially, in my own life it was profound. My purpose was to surrender to the joy of being—really being—with whomever I am with, instead of constantly thinking that I should be someplace else doing something different.

There is a phenomenon that I have come to call the *paradox of patience*. In the Ego Mind it is believed that if we are too patient we will miss something vital. Something important might happen when we are not present. The thought "if I hurry up to get there, I will arrive that much sooner" sticks in our mind. But the problem is that even when we hurry to get there, *"there"* never seems to arrive. We spend our lives rushing to a series of life-or-death appointments. But something quite remarkable and paradoxical occurs when we develop patience: *Patience produces immediate effects.* This is a paradox because it is with the attitude of patience that peace of mind is immediately experienced. A quote from *A Course in Miracles* illustrates:

> *Now you must learn that only infinite patience produces immediate effects. This is the way in which time is exchanged for eternity. Infinite patience calls upon infinite love, and by producing results* now *it renders time unnecessary.*

PATIENCE AND SITUATIONS— LETTING GO OF CONTROL

For much of my life my personal motto could have been, "Happiness is knowing what is going to happen next." I felt most comfortable when I was in control of situations. I feared any situation that might not have a controllable outcome that I could manipulate.

Many of my control issues began very young. Growing up in an alcoholic home, arguments that my parents sometimes had terrified me. Often, I felt the situation could easily escalate into something violent or an uncontrollable verbal attack I felt unsafe around. I felt unable to leave or control the situation.

Many people tend to want to minimize the effects of their childhood. Common minimizing statements include, "Well, I was never physically abused," or "It's all over now." It is important to allow ourselves to explore who we are, including who we were during our childhood, without limiting our understanding of it by predetermining what is "good or bad." Many of us have seen the horrible ways that children have been treated. We see television specials on abuse and say to ourselves, "How can I have problems with my parents when nothing close to *that* ever happened to me?" We must remember that it is our inner subjective experience that we are concerned with exploring. Comparisons limit this.

As a child, and later in adolescence, I tried to control my family conflicts and personal relationships by adopting various physical problems. Irrationally and unconsciously, I believed if I were physically ill, the focus of attention would be on me rather than any other conflict between my parents. I would thus be able to control potential conflicts. Whether feigned or organically based, I believe my physical problems emerged from feeling afraid of both conflict and intimacy, and wanting to have more control.

Fear and control are another one of the ego's damaging cycles. Fear often becomes manifest in the body. Many physical problems are actually based upon control issues, something I have seen on numerous occasions in the course of my work as a psychologist.

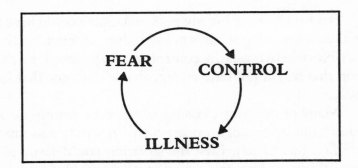

One such case involved Judy, a forty-seven-year old professional woman who appeared to have her life in good order. Judy had experienced a difficult and painful childhood. And because she was so successful financially, she believed her childhood was now of little consequence.

Judy was on her second marriage. Two days before our first meeting she had learned her husband was having an affair with her sister. And so it was that she came to see me in an emotional crisis, unable to work, sleep, or eat.

Judy revealed that her parents had divorced when she was fifteen. Their decision to divorce was a surprise to her. Her parents had never really had much of a relationship; they seldom showed emotion and were rarely together. Yet up until their separation Judy had never questioned her parent's relationship. She simply assumed it was a "normal" marriage.

Nevertheless, on a deeper level Judy had primarily felt unsafe in her family. She had not been supported in revealing her feelings about virtually anything. At the same time, Judy was never fully conscious of how emotions were denied in her family. She masked and repressed her feelings by doing well in school and gaining popularity among her peers.

When her parents divorced, nobody was able to talk about feelings. What Judy was feeling at the time was an overwhelming sense of being out of control and extreme anger towards her parents. Because expressing anger was clearly not permissible in her family, Judy's anger combined with feelings of loss of control, and at fourteen Judy virtually stopped eating—a dysfunctional way of dealing with the feelings exploding inside of her. Judy became obsessed with her weight, and began her way down the path to anorexia nervosa. Though she regained some of her normal body weight in her twenties, Judy still had the tendency to obsess about her weight. She had a difficult time with food and body image, especially in times of stress.

Judy's monetary success masked her internal struggle. She believed that if she were financially well off she would not need to face her emotional issues. Nobody ever questioned Judy's emotional health. Yet, the truth was that her internal feelings were marked by low self-esteem, lack of trust, and self-judgment, and had been throughout most of her life.

When Judy learned of her husband's affair with her sister, she became almost incapacitated with anger. She had no idea how to express this anger. She feared losing both relationships, yet at the same time could not see herself ever forgiving either of them. She began having difficulty sleeping and rarely ate any food. It was as if she could not accept any emotional nourishment for herself, and sleep and food metaphorically and symbolically represented this. She was taking her anger and directing it towards herself in an irrational and largely unconscious attempt to regain some control over her life. More specifically, Judy was wounding herself so that her husband and sister would see their "wrong." Judy was becoming a walking symbol of pain so that they would feel guilty. This was the only way she knew to control the situation. Obviously this was not resulting in any peace of mind for her.

In therapy, Judy was able to experience and communicate her anger. This led to her letting go of the anger rather than reinforcing it. With time she was able to relinquish the need to be controlling by working through much of the fear that she experienced as a child. She took the conscious decision to no longer make herself the "walking wounded" in an attempt to symbolically punish others. In short, Judy found that she did have a choice in how she felt, and realized that she could communicate those feelings in a direct and positive manner. This allowed her to begin to feel a sense of empowerment in her life that had previously escaped her.

Like Judy, as an adult I also became uncomfortable with spontaneity. I did not trust the unfolding of my life. I felt that knowing what was next, especially in terms of relationships, was of the utmost importance. I could never really comfortably walk through life and take joy in the spontaneous and creative aspects of existence. It was as though I were attending a play as a member of the audience, yet would repeatedly get up and try to direct the production. I was not ever fully satisfied with life. I thought if I could make every situation to my liking I would have happiness.

I found, however, that I was not happy. I needed to approach life quite differently. Being a student in *A Course in Miracles* assisted me greatly. I began to see that adopting an attitude of patience, based upon trust, yields the relinquishment of having to control. In relinquishing control we have a greater ability to be truly present with ourselves, others, and with life. True patience is outlined in the following.

THE FIVE PRINCIPLES
OF PATIENCE

1. Within every life situation there is a lesson to be learned. There is no such thing as a useless occurrence.
2. It is our subjective beliefs about a situation, not the objective facts of a particular situation, that determine what we experience.
3. Peace of mind comes from allowing ourselves to be in touch with all that we are. We do this by not placing limits, including time restraints, upon any aspect of ourselves.
4. To experience the most profound fragrance you would never rush a rose to bloom. Instead you would tend to the soil, prune dead leaves, and supply nutrients. Treat yourself in the same manner. Make sure you deal honestly with yourself and others. Let go of the past, and be loving and kind towards yourself and others.
5. Being internally focused brings peace. Being only externally motivated brings conflict. When in need of direction, your inner guidance will lead you to peace.

PATIENCE AND PEOPLE—
SEE A TEACHER IN EVERYBODY

It never ceases to amaze me how the Ego Mind can work its way into our thinking without our realizing it. I think I would notice if twenty or thirty uninvited guests showed up in my living room, but I don't always recognize fearful and shame-based thoughts in my mind.

I have made progress in becoming more aware of my negative thoughts, but I don't always catch them at the front door. Sometimes by the time I see them they are already making themselves at home. One of the sure signs that some uninvited thoughts are present in my mind is when I become short with another person—myself included. It may be the grocery clerk who is not ringing up items fast enough. It may be my wife while we're having a discussion. It may be that I think that I am making too many mistakes or taking too long at some task, and I begin to berate myself inside my head.

Whenever we become impatient with another person we are turning our back on a teacher that is there for the sole purpose of helping with our growth. This does not mean that everybody acts like a kind and compassionate third-grade teacher. In fact, some of our teachers come in less than desirable forms.

If you really want to develop patience, the important thing to remember is even those whom you find most unbearable have something to teach you. Perhaps you can learn about kindness. Obviously it is easy to be kind to someone who is nice and friendly, but it is not so easy to extend ourselves in kindness to someone who is, say, yelling at us. Remember, to have all that patience can offer us, you must be willing to be patient in all circumstances and with all people. You must have the *intention* to have boundless love and patience.

When I was in my first month of my first internship in clinical psychology a young man named Nathan came to see me professionally. Nathan was fifteen years old and had suffered moderate organic damage to both hemispheres of his brain. Two years before, a truck had struck him while he was riding his bicycle. His attention span was minimal. He often would lapse into very loud bursts of laughter, or would repeat one phrase repeatedly. The left side of Nathan's body was in partial paralysis, which caused a very noticeable and slow stride. But despite all of Nathan's organic damage, his personality could still be seen. Through the months, glimpses of the "whole Nathan" would reveal themselves.

To be quite honest, Nathan and I got off to a rather slow start. I was new to the job and not really sure what the heck I was supposed to do. I was very aware that both Nathan's and my own "progress" was going to be monitored by a supervisor. Frankly, I partly wanted him to do well so I would "look good."

As time went on I was able to let go of what "I was supposed to do" and became more present with Nathan. But everything that Nathan did took at least five times as long as it once would have. One of my tasks with Nathan was to help him become as self-sufficient as possible, for example, being able to go to the store without becoming confused, anxious, and disoriented. All of this took a great deal of time. In my increasingly busy schedule I started to feel resentful and angry that Nathan was not making much progress. I was mad at him for not getting better. I had a difficult time being patient with him when I felt like I had so many other things to do. Needless to say, when I had this attitude neither one of us ended up feeling very good.

By the time my one-year internship was complete Nathan had made very little progress. I believed this was due to the severity of his organic damage, and I did not think much about Nathan after that.

Many years later, at a restaurant in town, I saw Nathan and another person having lunch together. I did not recognize him at first because he was not displaying any of the behavior—the loud laughter and defiant attitude—that had so bothered me before. Nathan had gone to a group home which had one very remarkable counselor: the woman lunching with him that day. Marina had patiently spent a great deal of time with Nathan. Their relationship did not ride on any expectations of improvement.

While Nathan went to the rest room, I spoke with his counselor. It was clear that Marina really loved Nathan. She chose to identify with the little glimpses of the "whole Nathan" rather than trying to "fix" the "problem Nathan." I thought of the hundreds of hours that they must have spent together and thought how remarkable they both were.

I told the counselor how impressed I was with her. She said whatever patience she did have, Nathan had helped her with. Marina insisted that it was not her that was the "professor of patience," but rather it was Nathan. She said, "Can you imagine one day waking up and only being half as smart as you are now, and not being able to even tie your own shoes? Nathan is the teacher to *me*. I consider it an honor to spend time with him."

Nathan and his counselor, and countless others as well, have been great teachers to me about patience. Watching the two of them interact I could see a quality of patience and trust that seemed boundless. If I can remember the lessons they teach me, I will be well served.

THE LESSONS OF PATIENCE

- Whoever is in front of you is your teacher. We are all teachers and students to one another.
- Each moment you spend with another person is a precious gift. When you are with one person, try not to think you should be with someone else or someplace else.
- Look to the heart of a person rather than to their behavior. Heart to heart communication can transcend any impatience that you may have.
- Be gentle with yourself and you will move much further.
- Spend some time walking when you could run, sitting silently when you could stand and stew. Spend time listening when you could speak. Heal when you could harm. In these things you will find patience for yourself and others.

LESSON FIFTEEN

"Focusing on the present yields patience."

To be patient is to see all things through the perception of the present moment. To accurately perceive another person you must see them only as they are *now.* And this is equally true when looking at ourselves.

When we become impatient, we are, in fact, viewing life through past experiences or in anticipation of future ones. We are judging that the present moment should be different than it is rather than joyfully accepting life's unfolding.

The truth is that the "past has no reality in the present." Yet most of us consider it natural to use our past as the reference point in viewing the present. We believe it is natural to try to control the future in order to make our lives safe. Yet this idea is actually very *unnatural.* It is delusional. To understand patience we must look upon ourselves and others with no reference to the past. Then we will be able to learn from what we see.

Peace will be ours today as we focus upon the present. Patience is the miracle that occurs when we stop seeing the past and future as our only reality. We are fearful and controlling when we anticipate the future on the sole basis of our past experience. The result is always a conflicted mind. In contrast, when we allow the present moment to rise above the past and the future, we give ourselves freedom. We sever the chains that hold us back.

Patience is the opposite of condemnation. They cannot occur at the same time. Today focus on the present moment and find that patience brings you peace of mind. Should you be tempted to judge a situation, another person, or yourself, state clearly:

"Today I want to find the present.

I release _____ from the past."
(*Person, situation, myself*)

If you want to develop patience you must be willing to give up your judgmental thoughts and free yourself from the past. Ask yourself in all situations that you feel impatient in: Why would I hold the past against this person? Why would I want to keep this person in darkness by looking at them through the window of the past? Why would I refuse a teacher the opportunity to teach me?

LESSON SIXTEEN

"When I am healed I am not healed alone."

Patience and healing are intimately connected. So are sickness and fear. Patience brings healing to our minds. Sickness is a result of *separation*. At the root of patience is the knowledge that we are not separated from each other by anything but our thoughts. With patience we heal our minds from the belief that we are alone and isolated.

It may be helpful to specifically define healing: *Healing is the decision to be one again, and to accept ourselves and others as whole.* Because we all share an underlying common bond we cannot be healed alone. We cannot experience healing while believing that we are separate, better than, or less than. Patience is the foundation that allows healing to take place. It is the "holy land of the mind" that allows the truth about ourselves and others to emerge unmarred by the ego. To be healed is simply to accept the underlying unity that always has been, and always will be. Patience and healing can't occur alone; they happen simultaneously, which is what gives them truth. Healing, forgiveness, and patience are one, as are sickness, judgment, and fear.

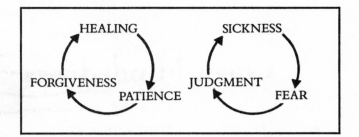

Healing is freedom,
and patience is the gentle path to healing.
Healing is strength,
and patience is the means by which we become
*   strong.*
Be patient and be healed.

Each person who is in your life offers you the opportunity for healing. When you adopt the attitude of patience you become capable of seeing the lessons that you once overlooked.

Today make the commitment to heal your mind. Know that you do not experience healing alone. Be thankful to every situation and to every person that enters your life today. Your gratitude will create patience. Avoid any temptation to judge. As every hour comes say to yourself:

> *"When I am healed I am not healed alone.*
> *Patience with myself and others will reveal*
> *a lesson for me to learn."*

A key factor in helping to develop patience is the breath. When you are calm and patient your breath is naturally fluid and deep. In contrast, when you are impatient and anxious your breath is short and shallow. Begin your hourly practice by focusing on your breathing. Consciously deepen and slow your breath. Should you find yourself "off track" during the day, before you even say the lesson to yourself spend a few seconds redirecting your breathing. Your breathing will help direct your ability to be patient.

Open-Mindedness

If you hold firmly to some set of beliefs or other,
you look at everything through that particular
prejudice or tradition; you don't have any contact
with reality . . . If you have no prejudice,
no bias, if you are open, then everything
around you becomes extraordinarily interesting,
tremendously alive.
J. Krishnamurti in
Think on These Things

To many of us, being open-minded is as for-
eign as some ancient tribal custom. Our Western industrialized
society places emphasis on teaching our young how to be critical,
analytical, comparative, objective, logical, and categorical. These
are the traits of an accomplished mind it is believed.

Of all of these characteristics, the word *objective* stands
out for me when I look at this list. Our society has become reliant
upon, if not addicted to, thinking that the objective is superior
over the subjective. How much money we have, for example,
or what kind of job we have, is valued more than the depth of
our inner experience of self. If we make a decision and someone
asks, "How did you decide that?" we feel compelled to provide a
chronology that documents our ability to think objectively. Those
who make decisions using their subjective experience are seen as
"intellectually weak." A man who says, "I hired this person for
the following five reasons," is seen as stronger than one who says
that he hired this person because of a connection felt with him or
her, an intuitive trust in this person.

To clarify, the *objective* is that which is external, measurable, and observable. The *subjective* are all of the internal experiences in which we live most intimately and genuinely. The subjective includes, but is not limited to, all of our emotions, perceptions, thoughts, feelings, intuitions, hunches, values, preferences, dreams, and all that makes each of us unique and wonderful, and this subjective experience is the main concern of this book. I believe the subjective is the source of our "aliveness." If we are to have richer and deeper lives we must abandon our addiction to objectifying the world and ourselves. We must make inroads to honoring the subjective.

The truth and depth about who we are lies in our subjective experience, the ebb and flow of our inner sea—a sea filled with depth and mystery. Our continued attempts to make ourselves an object and our universe finite only leads to denying our limitless depth.

When we are being open-minded we are believing in and focusing upon our subjective experience. The nature of subjectivity is as waves continually advancing and receding on the shore. Each wave is different than the last, and the shape of the shore is ever changing. If we believe that after watching a number of waves we understand the nature of all waves, we have made a mistake. In the same way, each moment brings with it a new, wonderful, and unique experience.

Let me clarify further: I believe that I know my wife, Carny, very well. She has been open and honest with me throughout our relationship. I have had the opportunity to come to know her family, and I know much about her childhood. When I think about it, I probably know thousands of details about her. Yet if I take this accumulated information and say to myself, "I now know Carny completely and totally," I have made a grave mistake. As are each of us, she is much more than an accumulation of information and experiences. In order to stay fresh and open-minded in my relationship with Carny, I try to always remember that I don't know the nature of the next wave no matter how long I have been sitting on the beach.

The Ego Mind uses our memory, which is selective, as a way of predicting the future and categorizing people. The result is that we are closed-minded. With objective data we begin to develop categories of information, or schemas. We then tend to want to fit new information into these schemas. The Ego Mind is much more concerned with figuring out the "cause" of a certain behavior than it is with experiencing the depth of who we are—that permeates our being.

Let us take the wave metaphor a bit further. In our Ego Mind we sit upon the beach and want to watch the waves and say, "Oh, look at that *big* one, look at that *pretty* one." We classify each wave. In contrast, the Whole Mind allows us to *experience* each wave as if it were a new phenomenon.

In Carmel, near where I now live, there is a man by the name of Max. When I was growing up I spent summers in Carmel, and even then Max was quite old. I was surprised a few years ago when Max came to visit me at the hospital where I am on medical staff. He had heard that I was back living in town and he wanted to visit me. I had not seen Max since I was about twelve. Amazingly, he looked exactly like he did before, over twenty years ago.

Max has walked on Carmel beach every day for over fifty years. Each day he tends to the beach as though it was his treasured back yard, lovingly picking up trash, smiling and talking to those he meets. Talking with Max at the hospital that day, I realized that his enthusiasm for life and the beach was remarkable and unique—much like that of a child going to the beach for the first time. He had nothing but open anticipation each time he went. I do not think Max ever saw the same shell, boulder, or shoreline in the same way twice. He always seems to have a "new mind" in how he approaches it.

From Max I learn about open-mindedness, and I learn about youth. Max shows me that youth has nothing to do with chronological age. Youth is the ability to walk through life with an open mind—with a listening ear to the subjective.

Disappointingly, many people are not happy, even though

they say that they desperately want to be. I believe they are unhappy for the simple reason that they are unaware of the love in their hearts. Max, as he walks his beach and smiles at each person he meets, teaches that love fills our hearts as soon as we remove the barriers between ourselves and other people or nature. When we cease to judge, and when we can simply enjoy the beauty of something without categorizing it, the main barriers disappear.

Most of us have a very difficult time with this. When we observe something, our minds always seem to want to make commentary about it: *"This is similar to the other one I saw." "This is of no use." "This is good, that is bad."* When we have an open mind we release it from all prejudice. We allow what we see to *describe itself to us,* rather than letting our preconceived thoughts and experiences define it.

I recently had an interesting lesson in this "mind as commentator" phenomenon. For a while I was living in a house where we had a satellite dish for television reception. At certain times the "news feeds" (the raw footage with no commentary by an anchorperson) would come over the air. I found that my mind was so used to being told what was going on and what to *see,* as in regular news broadcast, that I became easily bored with the news feeds. My mind had become quite lazy in just observing.

Open-mindedness occurs when we turn down the volume of our thoughts and experience what we are seeing. You might consider trying to develop your skills in observation and experience without commentary. It can be quite a difficult task for the mind that has become accustomed to constant input, but it is a most worthwhile skill to have. Just observe, experience, and discover.

By simply observing the trees, the animals, people talking, laughing, and crying, something quite remarkable happens deep inside us. What happens is that our hearts becomes activated. What we experience is from the heart rather than from the commentary of an always-busy intellect. When you are open and listening to the subjective, everything becomes miraculously interesting and amazingly alive.

OPEN-MINDEDNESS
AND ATTACHMENT

Did you ever look openly and honestly at how attached you may have become to people, beliefs, and material things in your life? It is difficult to do so because our Ego Mind tells us we dare not look at these attachments. It firmly holds that we need each and every one of them in order to be happy, and it fears any type of loss.

To be truly open-minded we must free ourselves from the attachments of the ego and heal our fear of loss. This is what we were doing in the first half of this book. We were determining what is valuable and what is not, and then letting go of what is not. How simple, yet how difficult when we believe in the Ego Mind.

Inordinate attachment happens when we think that some particular person, idea, ideology, or object will make us happy. This is not to say that open-mindedness and non-attachment mean isolation and discomfort. Non-attachment recognizes that once we are attached to having any particular thing we become a slave to it. We fear its loss, and our options of spontaneity and unencumbered choice diminish.

The mind that fears loss does not ever want to be questioned about its attachments. Attached to a particular level of comfort, a certain belief, an established habit, or even to a specific geographical location, it becomes encased in defenses. Ultimately it will do almost anything not to suffer loss. It is not really important what external trappings—clothes, car, house, and so on—your life has or doesn't have. What is important is developing an inner simplicity that allows your mind to be open and marvel at all creation. Attachment does not allow for this. With each attachment you move a little further away from the ability to experience the peace of mind that comes from inner simplicity.

Knowing inner simplicity gives us a feeling similar to the one we get from walking into a beautiful garden. Not an elaborate or ornate garden, just a beautifully simple one: cleanly raked, the flowers in bloom, perhaps a wind chime in the distance.

Inner simplicity rests in the mind not weighted down with resentments, or clogged with endless fears about the future. Fear of loss disappears once such simplicity is attained. The non-attached mind is free to genuinely think because it is not full of preconceived and rigid ideas. When we have a lot of attachments we have a difficult time discovering and exploring ourselves and our world. It is hard to travel into the depths of ourselves when we cling to our limiting beliefs.

HOW WE BECOME
CLOSED-MINDED AND CLOSED-HEARTED

If you take your hand and make a fist, closing it as tightly as possible, what do you feel as you look at it? Similarly, if you then relax the hand, making it as supple and open as possible, what do you feel? Can you feel the difference in these two postures, how they create two different experiences? It certainly takes more effort to keep one's hand tightly closed in a fist than it does relaxing it into an open palm.

The same is true of our minds. Parents and teachers rarely encourage us to think open-mindedly. Because of our experiences growing up, many of us have become used to having a closed mind. Yet we rarely question the energy that it takes to maintain it. Nothing depletes our energy more than being afraid. Being afraid always leads to a closed mind, which in turn leads to more fear—a cycle that builds upon itself like a snowball rolling downhill.

It is important to recognize the connection between having a closed mind and having a closed heart. When we begin to open our mind then there is room for broader and different perceptions: This in turn allows for our hearts to open. Closed-mindedness always leads to limiting our ability to have an open and loving heart. In becoming open-minded we are developing our capacity to give and receive love from the heart. Similarly, when we focus on opening our heart we are cutting through closed-mindedness.

As children grow up, it is crucial that they know that having *and* expressing feelings and thoughts is of the utmost importance. They need to be encouraged to explore and communicate the subjective aspects of who we are. Unfortunately, many parents actually douse the sparks of the subjective with water from their own wells of fear. The child hears, "Don't ever backtalk," "Do as I say, not as I do," "Shut up," "You don't know anything," "You're stupid," "Where do you get such dumb thoughts and ideas," "Who do you think you are?" These statements teach children to close their minds to their inner worlds.

The good news is that, as adults, we can unlearn old messages that caused us to close off. We can begin to open ourselves to the world of endless diversity that lives both within and around us.

Sally was thirty-six when she first came to my office. She and her boyfriend Sam were expecting a baby and she was having an inordinately difficult time making a decision about whether to get married. She had decided that she was going to keep the baby either way.

In our first session, Sally said that since her early adolescence, she had never been without a relationship for more than a couple of months. At this point she would begin to distance herself from the man she was with. This usually took the form of becoming argumentative.

When Sally came to see me she thought all she had to do was to determine if Sam was going to be a good husband and father. She began by reading a list she had written, which contained all of the positive and negative qualities he had. Indeed, she had come to me wanting my "professional opinion" on her odds of success—a sort of the prognosis of Sam's ability to meet her expectations.

From the outset it was clear that Sally had no notion of the reasons that led her to have so many serial monogamous relationships. During the course of our subsequent sessions she slowly began to see that her solution did not lie in simply determining Sam's fate as a good husband. Sally would have had to look hard at her own history and existence and become more in touch with her own inner life.

Until the age of twelve, she grew up in a family that seemed to be very supportive to the growth of Sally and her two brothers. Her father was a pediatrician and her mother a housewife. Both parents were attentive towards their children in a very genuine way. They weren't merely present at school functions and other activities of their children, they actively participated in most of the events. Feelings and emotions were expressed without judgment or fear of retaliation. Most punishments were appropriate and physical striking never occurred. Sally did moderately well in school and had many friends.

When she was twelve, however, with no warning or notice, her mother left the family. Sally was the youngest in the family, and at this time most of her brothers had gone to college. In leaving, her mother only said she needed to "find herself" and that she could not keep giving to the family. Sally only sporadically saw her mother over the next few years—sometimes as frequently as once a month, but their communication was always superficial compared to before. Meanwhile, Sally's father became quite depressed and was unable to meet Sally's emotional needs either.

Surprisingly, Sally did not act out in any way. Her grades in school continued to be good. She did not switch peer groups or begin using drugs. To the casual observer Sally would have looked just fine. However, Sally's internal life began to shift radically. She began to distance herself internally from everyone in her life. Unconsciously she believed that if her mother could just up and leave, anybody could. Because there was no warning before her mother's departure, Sally felt that there was no way of telling who could be trusted. She made the semi-conscious decision to never get too close with anybody.

As an adult, Sally began to feel anxious in her relationships with men at about the three-month mark, or when any depth or intimacy would begin to form. She never really questioned this; she assumed it was because she had not found the "right" person. Her way of guarding herself was to close herself off from deep feelings by being defensive. Sally did this by always finding fault in whoever she was with at the time. Her underlying fear of abandonment caused her to look at the world as a very unsafe place, a place where nobody can be counted on. Closed-mindedness took the form of being sure that all people would leave her, no matter how "good" they might be as a partner.

There are many different examples of the effects of closed-mindedness in relationships that we could cite that are quite different than Sally's. There are many things that lead us to being closed-minded. Many have to do with how our parents raised us, so each of us would do well to explore our own personal history. It is important to know, however, that the purpose is not to blame our parents. Our task is to begin to feel the impact of our childhood on our thinking today. The path to healthy relationships is not through blame, but rather through healing. Below are some of the main obstacles that we have to overcome in becoming more open. I have put them in the form of questions so you can begin to reflect on each of them. Note that the categories overlap in certain areas and some questions could appear in more than one area. No matter how many "yes" answers you give to the following questions, healing your heart and opening your mind is always possible.

EMOTIONAL GROWTH

1. Did you experience your parents as being emotionally inconsistent?
2. Were your parents sporadic in terms of support and discipline?
3. Were your parents nonsupportive of your individuality and uniqueness?
4. Was either of your parents chemically dependent?

5. Did either of your parents physically strike you?
6. Was either parent overprotective, controlling, or emotionally manipulative?
7. Was workaholism present in your family?
8. Was one parent overly dominant?
9. Did you witness spousal abuse between your parents?
10. Were you told not to cry, or were certain emotions seen as a sign of weakness?
11. Did either parent tend to rage or blow up with his or her anger?
12. Was physical affection generally withheld, or used in a manipulative or uncomfortable manner, in your family?
13. Did you feel that either parent was emotionally distant or unavailable most of the time?
14. Did you feel that you had to gauge what you said by the mood your parents were in?

INTELLECTUAL GROWTH

1. Was either of your parents rigid or prejudiced in his or her views of others?
2. Was either of your parents extremely opinionated, insinuating that other family members were stupid if they did not agree with him or her?
3. Did either parent put others down in order to feel superior?
4. Did your parents withhold encouragement and reinforcement when you expressed your opinions?
5. Did your parents show lack of approval when you expressed your own thoughts and ideas that differed from theirs?

6. Did your parents push you to an extreme to perform to certain high standards?
7. Were you ever called stupid or dumb?
8. Were the nonverbal messages in your family suggesting that you were different and didn't belong?
9. Were you embarrassed in school to talk in class? Did you fear having a wrong answer?
10. Did you tend to get in trouble if you challenged a parent or said no?
11. Were you afraid of one or both of your parents?

SOCIAL INTERACTION AND THE DEVELOPMENT OF HEALTHY SEXUALITY

1. Was either parent fearful of sexuality—either yours or theirs?
2. Did your parents have expectations on what "type" of friends and social life you should have?
3. Was either parent seductive towards you, either covertly or overtly?
4. Was either parent socially or monetarily competitive with others?
5. Was either parent racist or bigoted in any way?
6. Did your parents emphasize outer appearance more than inner feelings?
7. Was there a great deal of emphasis in your family on social status?
8. Were you ever shamed in public by either parent?
9. Was sex and sexuality never talked about in your family, or were they talked about only in joking or degrading ways?

10. Did your parents look to you to bring social acceptance to the family?
11. Was your choice of friends criticized on a continual basis?
12. Did either parent ever socially embarrass you?
13. Were you made to be afraid of other people or new situations?
14. When you made a mistake, were you usually met with ridicule or punishment?
15. Was being alone difficult for you?
16. Was being with others difficult for you?

SPIRITUAL GROWTH

1. In your family was one religion seen as superior to others?
2. Was God or spirituality denied in your family?
3. Was God used as a way to make you behave through fear of God?
4. Was the concept of sin used to induce guilt and control behavior?
5. Was morality used as a means to judge other people as being good or bad?
6. Were fear and intimidation used as forms of discipline?
7. Were you required to think and believe in a certain way about God and spirituality?
8. Were questions of a spiritual nature discouraged?

For every yes answer that you gave, you probably have some obstacles to overcome in working toward opening heart and mind. It is important for you to take some time on each of the yes answers. Write on it. Think about it. Feel it. Talk to friends. If you wish, enter psychotherapy. Perhaps talk with your parents.

The point is to begin to bring the aspects that lead to a closing of your heart and mind to your conscious awareness. The end goal is to let them go. For many of us this is neither an easy nor a brief process. It takes having faith that the journey towards openness is a worthwhile one. This book can help point you in the direction, but no book can take the place of the ongoing inner searching that is necessary for continuing our awareness and understanding of self.

I know that in my life I have found it necessary to continue to search my inner life and to be aware of aspects of myself that remain closed and afraid. Sometimes when I least expect it, a memory or feeling will surface that is another opportunity for me to learn. Often these are quite painful, yet working through them has always lead me to more openness and clarity.

I sometimes liken my own process to that of keeping my windows clean. It is a process that needs to be done on a continual basis. My history with my parents has yielded my fair share of yes answers to the above questions. After a lot of inner work I now feel my relationship with my parents is the best it has ever been, and I know that even more closeness is possible. Most importantly, this peace of mind has not been a result of my parents making amends for their "wrongs." It is a result of my working through the obstacles to openness that are in my life, and a result of forgiving.

LESSON SEVENTEEN

"I see nothing as it is now."

When we look through a tinted window, we see a tinted world. In this way, when we are looking through the lens of the past, we cannot see anything as it truly is *now* at this moment. This includes ourselves, others, the entire world. Most people have developed a habit of actually using their past experiences to determine the value of what is occurring in the present. In doing so they miss the essence of what they are experiencing.

Today, we look towards developing the skill of being open to the true nature of who or what is in front of us. The result will be a clear feeling of being more alive and awake in your life.

At first, the idea that what you see might not be there may sound like gibberish. To the untrained or closed mind, this concept can produce uncomfortable feelings. Indeed you *may* find yourself resistant to even entertaining such an idea because you have become so attached to seeing the world as you do. Fortunately, you do not have to worry about being resistant, or not understanding. The goal of each lesson is for you to *practice* applying the idea and to then *experience* the effects. Each minute that you practice today's lesson will open your mind a little more.

Today's exercises involve looking around you and applying the idea to all that you see. You needn't include everything, yet you must not consciously exclude anything or anyone. For example, you might look around say:

> *"I do not see this typewriter as it is now."*
> *"I do not see this telephone as it is now."*
> *"I do not see this arm as it is now."*

Four fifteen-minute practice periods are recommended today. Begin with things that are near to you and then gradually extend your range outward. If you wish, you may close your eyes and apply the lesson to whoever comes to mind.

> *"I do not see my mother as she is now."*
> *"I do not see myself as I am now."*
> *"I do not see my daughter as she is now."*

Say to yourself several times throughout your practice sessions:

> *"I want to see (this person or object) only as it is*
> *now, unencumbered by the past."*

LESSON EIGHTEEN

"I am determined to see things differently."

Today's lesson is a continuation and extension of the last one. Today more inner searching is done. Five practice periods of five minutes each would be ideal.

In each of the practice periods you may begin by repeating the lesson to yourself. Then close your eyes and search your mind for memories or situations in the past or the present, or anticipated events in the future, that bring up uncomfortable feelings for you. Try not to overlook anything, even if you feel it is only a mild annoyance. Sometimes you might want to dwell on certain memories, current situations, or people that seem to be more pressing or disturbing to you. During some of your practice periods, just before closing your eyes, you may want to read the questions that you answered yes to in the preceding questionnaire.

Remember that whatever comes to mind is subject to today's lesson. Don't worry if the subject seems insignificant to you. Also, you may come across angry and attacking thoughts. Today you have the opportunity for transformation. Be sure to include these as well.

As you search your mind for all obstacles to openness, hold each one in your mind as you say to yourself:

> "I am determined to see _____
> (name of person) differently."
> "I am determined to see _____
> (specify the situation) differently."

Feel free to expand on the lesson especially to create a positive alternative to painful experiences in your past. For example, after applying the above statement to the question, "Were your parents nonsupportive of your individuality and uniqueness?" you might add: "My uniqueness is important and deserves to be supported." This will plant the seed; the idea that you are whole and valuable.

You may want to spend more than just one day with today's lesson, because it takes great determination and practice to reverse our old ways of seeing things. Many people carry the weight of past situations from childhood to old age, never knowing the true extent to which they are being limited. How freeing it is today to begin to loosen all that holds you from being fully alive and realizing your full potential.

> *I am complete.*
> *I am full of love and potential.*
> *I am capable.*
> *Any thoughts other than these are false.*
> *Let me remember who I am today,*
> *And to light this memory in all whom I meet.*

EPILOGUE

This December morning a low winter sun casts shadows through old oak trees. On the gnarled branches some of the leaves appear dead, a result of last year's frost. Yet I can see new life growing side by side. In this way, the canopy displays the beautiful contrast of bright green growth against dusty brown.

These oaks remind me of my own experience writing this book. Though the overall process has been one of joy and learning, there have been slow times, frustrating and questioning points, dead ideas I hung on to, and even moments of inner despair. Nonetheless, as I read the pages back to myself, I too am struck by the new growth, the aliveness that I often felt along with my frustration. As with the oak leaves, a strange yet beautiful contrast.

In writing this book, I realized more than ever how I teach what I want to learn. I am still developing trust within myself. The writing of this book has helped me personally: I hope that you, the reader, have also benefited.

Existing within each moment of life is the possibility of trust, endless depth of feeling, and unconditional love. These are the treasures you deserve. It is your natural right to reclaim them.

May we each discover the depths of ourselves
by allowing trust to unfold within us,
and compassion to fill and heal our hearts.
May we each look to others as our brothers and
    sisters,
and treat them with kindness and dignity.

We are all—everyone of us—deserving of love,
at all times in all situations.
Withhold love from no living being.
Know, welcome, and share
the truth of who you are.

APPENDIX

LOCATION OF
QUOTES AND PARAPHRASES
IN *A COURSE IN MIRACLES*

All material quoted in *A Course in Miracles* can be located by referring to the following chart. The Second Edition of the Course was used. Quotes are listed in order of appearance in *The Art of Trust,* and some appear more than once. The following abbreviations are used in the chart.

T = Text   M = Manual for Teachers
W = Workbook for Students   p = Part   r = Review

Quote in *Art of Trust*	Section ACIM	Paragraph ACIM	Line No. ACIM
"The period of undoing."	M-4.I.A.	3	1
"The period of sorting out."	M-4.I.A.	4	1
"The period of relinquishment."	M-4.I.A.	5	1
"The period of settling down."	M-4.I.A.	6	1
"The period of unsettling."	M-4.I.A.	7	1
"The period of achievement."	M-4.I.A.	8	1
"There is another way of looking at the world."	W-p.I.33	Lesson	
"Forgiveness is the key to happiness."	W-p.I.121	Lesson	
"Period of Undoing"	M-4.I.A.	4	1
"Period of Sorting Out"	M-4.I.A.	4	1
"Minds are joined."	T-18.VI.	3	1
"Period of Relinquishment"	M-4.I.A.	5	1
"Above all else I want to see things differently."	W-p.I.28	Lesson	
"Above all else I want to see this table differently,"	W-p.I.28	2	1
"All fear is past and only love is here."	W-p.II.293	Lesson	
"The period of unsettling."	M-4.I.A.	7	1
"Period of Sorting Out."	M-4.I.A.	3	1
"Period of Relinquishment"	M-4.I.A.	5	1
"The period of unsettling."	M-4.I.A.	7	1

Quote in *Art of Trust*	Section ACIM	Paragraph ACIM	Line No. ACIM
'In the Period of Unsettling, which may take some time because it is so contrary to what many of us have learned, our goal becomes to lay all judgment aside. We can then ask our higher power for guidance in virtually every circumstance that presents itself to us. If each previous period were not heavily reinforced by greater feelings of peace of mind and a greater ability to trust, this task would be next to impossible.' (paraphrased)	M-4.I.A.	7	1-9
"the voice you choose to hear... depends entirely your whole belief in what you are."	T-21.V.	1	8-9
"There is another way of being in the world."	W-p.I.33	Lesson	
"The Voice of Love"	T-19.IV.D.	5	9
"Minds are joined."	T-18.VI.	3	1
"The period of achievement."	M-4.I.A.	8	1
"Forgiveness ends the dream of conflict here."	W-p.II.333	Lesson	
"Forgiveness is the light you choose to shine away all conflict and all doubt, ... No light but this can ... "	W-p.II.333	2	1-2
"Love holds no grievances."	W-p.I.68	Lesson	
"Love holds no grievances. When I let all my grievances go I will know I am perfectly safe."	W-p.I.68	6	8-9
"Love holds no grievances. Let me not betray my Self."	W-p.I.68	7	2-3
"To judge is to be dishonest, for to judge is to assume a position you do not have."	M-4.III	1	2
"To judge is to be dishonest"	M-4.III	1	2
"God's teachers do not judge."	M-4.III	1	1
"Judgment without self-deception is impossible."	M-4.III	1	3
"Judgment implies a lack of trust, and trust" 'is the foundation of the Whole Mind.' (single quotes is paraphrase)	M-4.III	1	6
"In fearlessness and love I spend today."	W-p.II.310	Lesson	
"Only my condemnation injures me."	W-p.I.198	Lesson	

Quote in *Art of Trust*	Section ACIM	Paragraph ACIM	Line No. ACIM
"Condemn and you are made a prisoner. Forgive and you are freed."	W-p.I.198	2	1-2
"Only my condemnation injures me. Only my own forgiveness sets me free."	W-p.I.198	9	3-4
"Let me be still and listen to the truth."	W-p.I.106	Lesson	
"Be still today and listen to the truth."	W-p.I.106	2	6
"I will be still and listen to the truth. What does it mean to give and to receive?"	W-p.I.106	7	5-6
"Truth will correct all errors in my mind."	W-p.I.107	Lesson	
"Light and joy and peace abide in me."	W-p.I.93	Lesson	
"Light, joy, and peace abide in you"	W-p.I.93	7	7
"Light, and joy and peace abide in you."	W-p.I.93	11	3
"it is not danger that comes when I lay down my defenses. It is safety. It is peace of mind. It is joy."	M-4.IV.	1	11-14
"The truth is that you are responsible for what you think, because it is only at this level that you can exercise choice."	T-2.VI.	2	6
"There is another way of looking at the world."	W-p.I.33	Lesson	
"Love is the way I walk in gratitude."	W-p.II.95	Lesson	
'Today walk in gratitude to the one force that ends all suffering; love.' (paraphrased)	W-p.I.r.VI.215	1	1
'walk in gratitude, the way of love.' (paraphrased)	W-p.I.r.VI.215	1	1
"It can be but my gratitude I earn."	W-p.I.197	Lesson	
'With such a world view, generosity comes to mean "giving away" in the sense of losing something.' (paraphrased)	M-4.VII.	1	4
'We give away in order to keep.' (paraphrased)	T-7.VIII.	1	6
"To give and to receive are one in truth."	W-p.I.108	Lesson	
"giving and receiving are the same"	T-25.IX	10	6
"To give and to receive are one in truth. I will receive what I am giving now."	W-p.I.108	8	2-3
"To everyone I offer quietness." "To everyone I offer peace of mind." "To everyone I offer gentleness."	W-p.I.108	8	6-8
"Truth will correct all errors in my mind."	W-p.I.107	Lesson	

Quote in *Art of Trust*	Section ACIM	Paragraph ACIM	Line No. ACIM
"Those who are certain of the outcome can afford to wait, and wait without anxiety... The time will be as right as is the answer. And this is true for everything that happens now or in the future."	M–4.VIII.	1	1,4,5
"I am here only to be truly helpful. I am here to represent Him Who sent me. I do not have to worry about what to say or what to do, because He Who sent me will direct me. I am content to be wherever He wishes, knowing He goes there with me. I will be healed as I let Him teach me to heal."	T-2.V.A.18	8	2-3
"... past has no reality in the present."	T-13.VI	1	4
"When I am healed I am not healed alone."	W-p.I.137	Lesson	
"I see nothing as it is now."	W-p.I.9	Lesson	
"I do not see this typewriter as it is now."			
"I do not see this telephone as it is now."			
"I do not see this arm as it is now."	W-p.I.9	3	3-5
"I am determined to see things differently."	W-p.I.21	Lesson	
"I am determined to see _____ (name of person) differently." "I am determined to see _____ (specify the situation) differently."	W-p.I.21	4	1-3